Contents

Introduction

I love working with babies and young children. They see the wonder in everything, so as a storyteller it's easy to make things fun and interesting. But as a parent it can be hard to find the time to spend introducing your child to new and exciting worlds. It's an exhausting job, and by the time you're ready for a bedtime read, it's more about bonding with your baby, and settling them down so that you can both have some much-deserved rest.

I wanted to write this book to show you how you can get so much more out of picture books using everyday toys and imaginative play. Of course, there is nothing wrong with just reading a book over again because babies love that. They need that familiarity and repetition so that they can start making connections between words and pictures and understanding what things mean. But it's also a good idea to vary things, and to get as much out of a story as you can.

Starting with a story

Try to see pictures books as a starting point for exploring new language and having lots of fun. That's the key. If you enjoy the activities in this book then your baby will enjoy them too. It's about the experience of sharing, and spending time together, but there's also no reason why you can't introduce a bit of learning and development into things. It's a fact that we learn more when we're enjoying ourselves, and stories are wonderful teaching aids.

When we listen to a story, we absorb more information because our brainwaves change. We become like human sponges, ready to connect with what is being said, and to identify with the content of the tale. Small children might not fully understand the words or the gist of the story, but they will still appreciate the experience, and will start to make those essential connections as their language develops.

READ ME A STORY

Help your child fall in love with books

Alison Davies

With foreword by
Nick Sharratt

Published 2011 by A & C Black Publishers Ltd
36 Soho Square, London W1D 3QY
www.acblack.com

ISBN 978-1-4081-326-47
Copyright © 2011 A&C Black Publishers Limited
Design © Lynda Murray 2011
Photos © Shutterstock and © Fotolia
Cover photograph © Shutterstock

A CIP record for this publication is available from the British
Library.

Printed and bound by Star Standard, Singapore

This book is produced using paper that is made from wood
grown in managed, sustainable forests. It is natural, renewable
and recyclable. The logging and manufacturing processes
conform to the environmental regulations of the country of
origin.

To see our full range of titles visit **www.acblack.com**

Foreword

Over the years I've been involved in creating all kinds
of children's books for every age range, and what
I've enjoyed more than anything else is producing
picture books. It's just the most delightful field to work
in, whether I'm providing images to go with another
writer's words or wearing my author/illustrator hat and
doing the whole thing myself. I'm given thirty two lovely
big pages in which I'm allowed to let my imagination
run riot, and rather wonderfully the more fun I can have
along the way, the better the book that will result. Then
when I've finished, there's the thrill of sharing my book
with its intended audience of little ones. I never cease
to be amazed by the extraordinary receptiveness of
very young children, their joy in new experiences and
their thirst to discover more about life. Picture books
can help them with this. If I've done my job properly
their wide-eyed absorption in the narrative, intense
fascination in the illustration and peals of laughter
at the humour will let me know that my book has
made a true connection and has in some way added
to their lives. That, quite simply, is what being the
creator of children's books is all about.

Now Alison Davies has had the marvellous idea
to write 'Read me a story', a brilliant guide to
understanding just how picture books work and how
to get the very best out of them. It's chock-a-block
with information, advice and great tips to help you
enjoy to the full the life-enhancing rewards that can
be achieved when a book is shared between an
adult and a tiny child.

Nick Sharratt

Regular routine

Establish a routine so that you have a regular time slot to spend reading with your baby every day. It doesn't matter if it's only ten minutes, this time will be important to you both. Use it for reading related activities, so that your baby gets into the habit of knowing that books are fun. Mix and match ideas from this book, and don't be afraid to repeat things. I've tried to build in activities that you can come back to over a period of time so that as your baby grows he will be able to contribute more, and get different things from the experience.

The idea is that picture books aren't just for babies. You don't have to put them away once your child reaches two or three, in fact you can use them right up until school and they will become much loved tools for you both.

Types of books

The pictures books I've chosen are some of the best out there. I've included a mix of classics that we all know and love and new books with a different energy and feel to them. Again the important thing is that you both like the look and feel of the book and enjoy reading it. When you've done this a few times, you might like to try some of my suggestions. I've put in ideas that can be used with babies and also children up to five years old, to give you a flavour of how things might develop as your child grows.

I've also included a section on stories that teach. These are tales that you can use when you want to introduce your child to change, or help them with a specific situation. Again these ideas are meant to be fun, and you may find that you want to adapt them to suit your needs. There are also suggestions for different types of storytelling games and activities – you need never be at a loss for something to do on a rainy day!

Activity ideas

Don't be afraid to experiment with my suggestions. Do what works for you. Your child is an individual and will respond differently to the activities, so the most important thing is to take their lead. See how they engage with the book. With babies, look out for tell-tale signs like lots of movement, wanting to touch pages and get involved. If they're making lots of noise that's generally a sign that they are trying to join in, but if their eye contact moves elsewhere, then maybe it's time to put the book away.

Don't persist with things if your child is not interested. At the end of the day it's about them having fun, and you enjoying your time together. Forcing your child to learn could have the opposite effect and turn them off books completely.

As you work your way through this book you'll see how easy it is to come up with fun games and activities related to stories. Be creative, and have a go with one of your favourite books. The one thing most picture books have in common is colourful illustrations that match the text and explain its meaning clearly. Make the most of this, and describe everything you see.

Creating stories

Once you feel confident with this, have a go at picking a character and making up a different story about them. Talk about key words as you go along and refer back to the book for information. You will find that as you deviate from the book more ideas will come, and soon you'll be playing storytelling games, and making up rhymes and riddles that you can use any time.

My hope is that this book will give you a wealth of ideas that are easy to run with and fun to do. You can either read this book from start to finish or dip into it at anytime for inspiration. Remember stories are a part of who we are. They are around us from day one, and they continue to be an important part of who we are, as we grow to adulthood. Take every opportunity to get creative with your child. See things through their eyes, and help them experience the wonder of the world and learn important life skills at the same time. Happy reading and learning!

Modern picture books

They say a picture paints a thousand words, and it's true. We connect to images on a deep level. They trigger something primordial, an understanding and a range of emotions that help us make sense of the world. This is something we never grow out of.

Think for a minute about a happy time in your life. It's impossible to recall the memory without seeing it as a picture, or running through the event like a film. This is because we need the image to help us connect to the emotion, to relive it and make it real. This is why picture books work so well with babies and young children. The picture captures their imagination. The book becomes a tool for learning, because they can reach out and experience the story. They start to recognise the patterns and shapes of words. Through facial expression and the tone of your voice they begin to understand what is happening.

You can take this a step further, by coming up with activities that are related to the story, and that's what this chapter is all about. I've selected some of the best new picture books on the market, and I've linked in some creative ideas that you can use. Remember, the secret is to have fun with this. Once you get started you will find you have your own ideas, and that each picture book becomes a springboard to learning.

A Head Full of Stories

by Su Swallow and Tim Archbold (Evans)

This book is easy to read, with lovely colourful illustrations that really add to the story. It's a simple tale about a boy (Jack) whose head is full of stories. He enjoys telling tales as much as reading them, and there's a funny twist at the end which small children will appreciate. Because the book refers to many classic fairy tales it has great potential for some fun follow-up activities.

Picture this!

As the story progresses, Jack goes to each member of his family and tells them a story. To complement this, the opposite page reveals a colourful picture to give the reader a clue as to what it might be.

- Use the pictures for some impromptu storytelling. It doesn't matter if your child doesn't know the fairy tale it's referring to – it's often more fun to make up your own. Start with the first picture about Cinderella. Point out the characters. Who are the two girls and why do they look so unhappy? Why is the smaller girl carrying clothes? What about the fairy, do you think she's come to help?

- Babies love sing-song language and even if they can't understand all the words, they will appreciate the rhythm and enjoy gazing at the pictures.

- Make this fun by turning it into a rhyme. Start with something simple like: *'Here's a girl with lots of clothes, she carries them everywhere she goes!'* or *'There's a fairy in the air, I wonder why she's hanging there?'*

Family fun

In the story Jack includes his family, his pet cat, and also his favourite bear. Small children love it when you put them in a story, and also include things and people that they are familiar with.

- Have a go at making up a story using family members, favourite toys and pets. You might say:

    "There's baby Tom sitting on Grandpa Joe's lap in the garden. It's a lovely sunny day and mummy is hanging out the washing. Timmy the dog is digging a hole."

Keep it simple, and make the exercise more about describing the pictures in the book and talking about things your baby can associate with. Look at the pictures together and talk about the details.

- With a slightly older child, ask her to draw a picture, and put in all her favourite things and people. Encourage her to describe the sounds, so for example, Timmy's yelping and barking, perhaps Mummy is singing a song and Grandpa is snoring.

- Ask your child which fairy tale they would read to each family member and why?

A dog's tale

At the end of the book there's a picture of everyone asleep except Jack and the dog, so there's no-one left to tell him a story. Or is there? Use the picture to help with some role reversal. Imagine if the dog could talk.

- Ask your child to think about what the dog would say if it could talk? What would its tale be? Perhaps it would be a story about a magic bone, or maybe the dog has his own adventure playing in the park?

- Ask your child to give the dog a name. What kinds of things does he like to do? Go back through the book together and look at the pictures. You'll see the dog having fun with Jack, playing with a ball, and jumping up and down. Together make up a short tale about the dog especially for Jack.

Charlie and Lola – I Am Really REALLY Concentrating

by Lauren Child (Puffin)

This book is a wonderful example of Charlie and Lola at its best. Fabulous illustrations mix with witty dialogue that captures the imagination. The story centres on school sports day, and Lola's struggle to find an event that she is good at. There are plenty of opportunities to join in, point things out in the text, and make this a fun learning experience for your child.

The octopus race!

' "Octopus Race?" says Lola. "What is an Octopus Race?" '

- Use this to launch into a new story about an 'Animal Sports Day'. Suggest that every year there's a special sporting event for animals. Help your child to imagine this by listing the animals that might be involved.

- Describe the line-up and the types of events they could enter. For example, there might be a banana race for monkeys, a stretching game for giraffes and a somersaulting race for dolphins. What about the octopus, what kind of race would he be good at, perhaps a tying shoe-laces race? Have fun with this and be creative.

- Ask your child to help by drawing a picture of 'Animal Sports Day' and together you can come up with a new tale that you can use in story sessions and keep adding to.

Sports day ditty

You can do this activity with a slightly older child.

- Focus on some of the action words in the story, like running, jumping, skipping and so on. Explain to your child that you're going to make up a sports day rhyme together.

- Start by asking them to repeat some of the action words. What do they sound like? Talk about what they mean.

- Now ask them if they can come up with other action words that rhyme and might add something to the poem. For example, jumping and bumping, or bouncing and pouncing. Make a list of these words together and have fun chanting them.

- Once you have a few rhyming words, you are ready to start the ditty. Remember to include your child by using their name. So you might say:

  'Sam goes skipping, zipping, nipping across the grass, while bouncing and pouncing upon the ball. Now he's hula hooping and loop the looping!'

- Encourage your child to join in with actions, and add any words or ideas to the rhyme.

Cupboard counting

At the beginning of the story Charlie goes through some sports ideas with Lola. On page three you'll see a picture of different types of sporting equipment in the cupboard.

- Get your child to count these with you, and go through what each one is, for example, 'This is a ball, we kick a ball.' Then come up with a little action for each that you can have a go at together. Eventually your child will associate the actions with the objects and this will help them make connections and understand what they're used for.

Click Clack Crocodile's Back

by Kathryn White and Joelle Dreidemy (Little Tiger Press)

This book is filled with lovely rhymes that you can enjoy together. The story is clever and funny, and you will both appreciate the twist at the end of the tale. There are lots of interesting animals in the book, and some exciting rhyming words and sounds that will really bring your storytelling session alive. Enjoy the story as a straightforward read, or use the book as a prompt for making up your own rhymes and discussing the different types of animals that you might find in the jungle.

Pick and mix words

In the book certain words are highlighted in bold.

- Make a list of the words in bold and come up with new words that sound like them, or fit together in a rhyme. For example you might take 'snaffle' and 'gobble' and come up with 'raffle' and 'bobble'.

- When you have a selection of these words, have a go at making up a rhyme using them. Use characters from the book, or make up your own scenarios. It doesn't matter how silly the rhyme is, the point of the activity is to introduce interesting sounding words to your child.

- If you can think of actions to go with the words, use them in your rhyme and encourage your child to join in.

Coloured creatures

Once you have read through the book and the rhymes have a go at counting the different animals in the book.

- As you count with your child look at the colours too, and make a connection between the two. So you might say, 'How many animals live in this book? Oh look, we have one green crocodile, two pink flamingos, one brown monkey,' and so on. When you have been through this a few times pointing out the animals and the colours, encourage your child to have a go.

- Now help your child to think about the sounds the animals make and include this in the activity. If she's old enough she might want to draw pictures of the groups of animals. Encourage her to think of other animals that might live in the jungle, and introduce a different number like 'three black panthers or four grey elephants'.

13

Dogs

by Emily Gravett (Macmillan Children's Books)

This beautifully illustrated picture book includes every type of dog you can imagine, with some lovely images, and a melodic text. It's easy to read and fun to share with young children. It introduces some nice descriptive words and there's a fun twist at the end.

Spot the mutt!

There are so many different types of dogs in this book that it makes a fun counting game.

- As you read the book count each dog that you see. As you turn the page and read out the text, recap on how many dogs you've seen so far. Repeat this with every new page, and point out the dogs.

- With tiny babies take their hand and help them trace the outline of each drawing.

- Encourage an older child to match descriptive words to the pictures. He can either use the ones provided by Emily, or add in his own. For example, the spotty dog could also be 'dotty' or 'blotchy', and the hairy dog could also be 'furry' or 'soft'. Take each dog and together make lists of words to describe them.

- When you've finished the book ask your child to pick out the dog they like the best and to tell you why.

Dog tales

This an idea to try with babies and slightly older children.

- With your child, open the pages of the book randomly and pick a dog. As you look at the picture think of a name for the dog, and have a go at telling its story. This doesn't have to be complicated. Start by talking about where the dog lives and what it likes to do. If it helps, have a list of questions to hand. Who does it live with, and where does it like to go? What does it like to eat for breakfast? Make up a day in the life of this dog and encourage your child to join in.

- Together decide upon a friend for the dog, and its favourite place and then have a go at drawing a picture. If you have your own dog, make connections by saying *'This dog looks a bit like our dog Sam, because it's small and hairy'*. This will help your child learn about the meanings of words and associate them with things she knows.

Woof woof!

- Together, think of all the noises a dog makes. Encourage your child to have a go at barking, going 'woof', snarling, howling, rolling around on the floor and scampering on all fours. This is great fun and really triggers the imagination.

- To get into character, make a dog mask by sticking bits of fake fur on to paper, cutting out holes for eyes, and adding in a big mouth. Take it in turns to wear the mask and play at being the dog!

Elephant Wellyphant

by Nick Sharratt (Alison Green Books)

This book is truly elephantastic! There are wonderful illustrations, ridiculous rhymes and opportunities for lots of repetition. This is perfect for babies and toddlers. It encourages them to have fun with made-up words and explore language, using sounds and rhyming words.

A day in the life...

Elephant Wellyphant is not a story book in the traditional sense, but you can use it to make up stories that your child will enjoy.

- Pick one of the made-up elephants in the book, for example *Polka Dot Umbrellaphant*, and create a short tale about a day in the life of this Umbrellaphant.

- Perhaps she lives in Umbrella World where it always rains, and one day *Polka Dot Umbrellaphant* decides that she's had enough of rain and wants to go somewhere sunny. She makes a wish, and suddenly her umbrella starts to zoom up into the sky taking her with it. Eventually she finds herself in a sunny place with lots of other elephants. That's when she realises she's in the pages of a colourful picture book.

Spot the word

- Pick a magic word from the book and tell your child that they have to listen out for it. When they hear or see the word, they have to shout it out loud three times or clap their hands.

- Do this regularly so that your child gets used to listening carefully to sounds and looking at the shape of words.

Create a character

- If your child is old enough, encourage her to have a go at making up a new elephant character. Ask her to think about the kinds of things she enjoys doing. Perhaps she has a favourite cuddly toy or bear that she plays with so you could suggest a 'Furry Bellyphant'? Or if she enjoys trips to the beach then a 'Seaside Shellyphant'.

- Ask her where this new character lives, and what she thinks it has for breakfast. Allow her to have fun with this. Help her draw her made-up elephant. Every time you read the book together, get out the pictures and run through the new characters, adding in more detail.

Gilbert, the Surfer Dude

by Diane deGroat (Harper Collins)

This book is part of the *I Can Read* series and is suggested as a 'Reading with help' book. The story features a little character called Gilbert the possum and his family. It has colourful illustrations, easy-to-read text, and the feel of a more grown-up book, which is great for small children just starting to recognise words. It gives them a sense of achievement, as they progress from just looking at the pictures to holding the book, and repeating sentences.

The story is about a trip to the seaside, where Gilbert becomes a surfer dude and rides the waves. There's a funny twist in the tale that young children will love, and the book shows Gilbert and his sister Lola overcoming their fears of the sea.

What's in the sea?

In the story Lola is afraid of the sea. Even though she has a nice new swimming costume, she doesn't want to go into the water because she thinks there are all sorts of scary things lurking there.

- Address this issue by talking about what could be in the water. Lola mentions sharks and jellyfish, but there are other things too.

- Make up a page of drawings yourself, by tracing pictures of underwater creatures, then together you can colour them in and talk about what they might be and what they do.

- When your child has a grasp of the names and shapes ask her to draw her own underwater scene, putting in all the creatures she can remember, and making it look colourful and magical.

Sea tales

- Make up an enchanting sea tale. Start by using an underwater setting. Pick a character to tell the tale for you, such as a little fish or a seahorse. Add an element of fantasy by thinking about all the magical creatures that might live in the sea such as mermaids and sea serpents.

- Introduce this underwater world to your child bit by bit, talking about how pretty it is. Talk about the colours and shapes. Try telling this story when your child is in the bath, so that you can pretend that the bath water is the sea. Say *'Today we're going to imagine that we're going for a swim in the sea. What shapes can we see beneath the water?'*

- Get pieces of blue card and cut out shapes of fish, or use bath toys as part of the story.

Seaside fun

Think about all the fun things you can do in the sea. In the book, Gilbert longs to be a surfer dude riding the waves, so you can mention this, and then talk about other activities.

- Talk about playing ball on the beach and try throwing a soft ball to each other.

- Remember to also talk about what the sea looks like. The foamy waves might look like white horses, or snow capped mountains.

- Use bubbles in the bath to draw comparisons and encourage your child to splash around and have fun. Soon she will realise that water is a good thing, and you will be able to introduce her to paddling and swimming pools.

Gruff the Grump

by Steve Smallman and Cee Biscoe (Little Tiger Press)

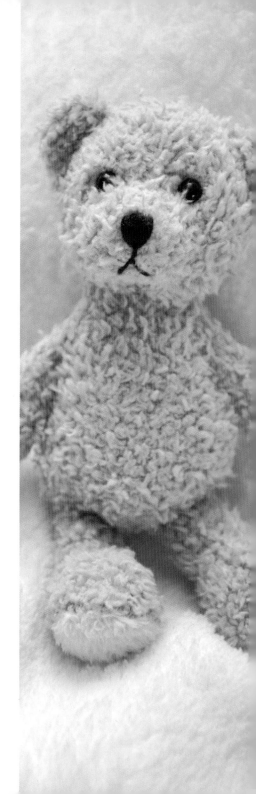

This charming picture book has a lovely message. It's all about friendship and kindness. Gruff the bear is a miserable grumpy bear who doesn't have any friends, until one morning along comes a little rabbit who is determined to make him smile. This book has gorgeous illustrations and a story that your children will fall in love with. It also offers plenty of potential for introducing fun activities and important life lessons.

Add a word

The story starts with a description of Gruff. *'Gruff was a bear. A great big bear. A great big, scowly, growly, grizzly grump of a bear.'*

- This lovely rhythmic use of language is an excellent starting point for exploring descriptive words. With your baby, simply repeat the sentence, adding in a new descriptive word every time. So you might say, *'A great big, hefty, scowly, growly, grizzly grump of a bear.'* Then the next time you might add in 'lumpy' or 'grotty,' or 'snarly' until you have a long list of words. Babies love this kind of chanting repetition.

- Encourage an older child to join in the process. Talk about the sort of words that you might include and what they mean. What does Gruff look like? Point out not just the way he appears but also his facial expression and what this means.

- When you have finished describing Gruff, do the same thing with his cave, or some of the other characters like the little rabbit. This is an ongoing process and a tool you can use with lots of picture books to build up a range of interesting words!

Box of surprises

In the book the little rabbit believes she's collecting golden stars, which turn out to be leaves.

- Have a go at drawing some leaf shapes and encourage your child to colour them in. What do they look like? What else might they be? Perhaps they are magic? Cut out the shapes and decorate them, or make up a colourful collage.

- Try collecting leaves with your child, and stick them on paper. Come up with ideas for how you might use them.

- To follow on from this go out into the garden or park and collect other natural objects that you could use, or describe in new and exciting ways. For example, you might pick a large smooth stone that you can paint and then use in a story, or a pine cone that you could spray and cover with glitter.

- Experiment with mud, and grass and use twigs in collages.

- Create a box of magical gifts from nature, and include some of your finds. Use this as a prompt for storytelling ideas by dipping into the box and making up a story about whatever you pull out. As your child grows up he will be able to join in and use the box in the same way.

Hooray for Fish

by Lucy Cousins (Walker Books Ltd)

This delightful board book is a must for all babies. The pictures are bright and illustrate the text perfectly and the text is light hearted and rhythmic, so it's easy to chant and repeat over and over again. Small children will enjoy discovering the different types of fish, and counting and describing them. There's plenty of potential for further activities and developing your own 'fishy' characters and tales.

Name the fish!

There are so many types of fish in this book, and particularly on the page where it says *'How many can you see?'* Lucy Cousins has cleverly come up with fish that look like insects, flowers and fruit among other things.

- Point at each fish and try to come up with ideas of what it looks like. You might think the two stripy blue fish swimming next to each other look like socks, or the thin blue and yellow fish looks like a snake or a scarf. Suggest as many alternatives as you can.

- Next, encourage your child to think of a name for each fish. The fish that resembles a strawberry might be called 'Berry'. Have fun with this and make up characters for them.

Fishy tales

- Now together have a go at making up your own fish. This can be as imaginative and silly as you like. Ask your child what kind of fish they would like to create. Encourage him to think about the kinds of things he enjoys doing and include some of these ideas in your creation. You might have a fish that looks like an ice lolly, or one that resembles a football!

- Give the fish a name and make up a fishy tale to go with it. Consider how your fish moves in the sea. Does it float, swim, splash, paddle or perhaps it can fly? Let your imaginations go and see what you can come up with together. Before you know it you'll have a whole deep sea world of amazing creatures!

Fish decorations

- If you're feeling really creative, try making a dangling fish decoration that you can hang from the ceiling in the bathroom. Cut some card into the shape of your fish, stick a piece of string to this with sticky tape then hang this from your ceiling. Use it in storytime sessions while your child is in the bath.

Hooray for Everything!

- Use the book as a starting point to develop your own tales about other creatures. For example, have a 'Hooray for Cats' book or a 'Hooray for Spiders' story.

- Take a creature, and come up with lots of different variations. Use Lucy Cousins' book as a starting point and make a note of all the different types of fish on every page. Go through them together pointing out the colour, size, shape and what makes them unique.

- Repeat the words so that your child has a chance to learn them and grasp the meaning. Now use the same words to come up with different types of cat, dog, spider, bird and so on. If your child is old enough ask her to illustrate your creations, until together you've come up with your own 'Hooray for...' tale.

Mouse and Elephant

by An Vrombaut (Hodder Children's Books)

This charming little picture book is a simple tale of friendship and fun. Mouse and Elephant want to play together, but they have to find something that they can do easily and that they both enjoy. They go through a range of different activities until Elephant comes up with the idea of creating a tricycle for two. The pictures are delightful and easy for young minds to understand.

Tap and clap

Each page mentions a new activity that Mouse and Elephant can do together.

- Use this as a starting point to think of action words associated with the activity. For example, basketball might be bouncing, thudding, shooting and scoring. Flying a kite might be swinging, swaying, dipping and soaring.

- If your child is old enough, encourage him to have a go at saying some of the words and adding in movement. Keep action words in groups of four to start with to develop a rhythmic flow:

What are Mouse and Elephant up to now?

They're bouncing, thudding, shooting, scoring – playing basketball!

What are Mouse and Elephant up to now?

They're swinging, swaying, dipping, soaring – flying a kite!

- Tap out the rhythm of the words with your hands, or clap and encourage your child to join in. Repeat as often as you like and add in more games and activities as you go along.

Look and see

The pictures in the book are very clever. Not only do they show what the activities are, but they also have lots of other things going on. When you look at the page about tightrope walking, you will also see that there are lots of other things in the sky, like birds, aeroplanes and helicopters. Even the birds are different, some are carrying things.

- Point these things out to your baby. Describe each one and include it in the story. Where there is more than one of any item, use it as an opportunity to count.

- If the pictures include things that your baby sees every day point this out. For example, you might say, *'Oh look a bird, just like the birds we see in the garden,'* and then show your baby a bird in the garden. This will help him to make connections with words and start to understand what they mean.

- As your baby gets older go through the book together and ask him what he can see in the picture. He will then be in the habit of looking closely and describing the illustrations.

What happens next?

- Play a game. What happens next in the story? Mouse and Elephant are on their tricycle and they've gone up the hill and over the edge. What do they see? Where will they be? Who will they meet? Come up with ideas together and encourage your child to draw you a colourful picture.

On the Farm

by Bénédicte Guettier (Zero to Ten)

This is another book in the popular *Funny Faces* series. Just like all the others, it has peep holes that you and your child can use to help tell the tale and become the animal characters. The illustrations are bright and the text is simple enough for young children to understand. Each page highlights a different farm animal and gives a brief description of what they might be doing. These actions and sounds are easy to repeat, and a great way to introduce new language to your child.

Farmyard tales

- Go through the book taking each page and becoming the animal character. Talk about what happens next. So if it says that the dog is sleeping, think about what might happen if the cow made a loud 'mooing' sound and woke him up. What would he do next? He might bark. He might chase the cow. Or he might just go back to sleep again! Take each page and create miniature farmyard tales together.

- Concentrate on one animal a day. So rather than going through the entire book, pick an animal, and spend the day doing things associated with that animal. Make the animal sounds, draw pictures, make up rhymes and stories, and become that creature for the day!

- Think about where the animals live, what they eat and create a little home for them in your play area. If you choose the pig, then you might build a comfy sty, and pretend to roll about in mud.

- Tell the story of *The Three Little Pigs*, or find other stories that you can use, as long as they have a 'piggy' theme.

- Make up a pig rhyme or a song about a little pink pig. Have fun with this and really let your imagination run riot. Remember that your child will learn by watching what you do. If he sees you getting into this activity and getting creative, he will realise that it's ok to do the same thing, and learn through play.

Farm fun

- As a follow-on from the book, think about who else might live on the farm. Talk about the farmer, his wife and the farm dog. Think about things the farmer uses in his work, like a tractor, or a plough and what types of noises they make.

- Imagine that you are adding pages to the book and together draw pictures with peep holes for the new characters. You might draw the tractor and cut out a hole where the farmer's head could appear. Use this together to imagine that you are riding on the tractor and exploring the farm.

One Mole Digging a Hole

by Julia Donaldson and Nick Sharratt
(Macmillan Children's Books)

This lovely rhyming picture book has lots of quirky ideas that your child will love! It is funny and a little bit silly, with lots of actions, words and things to pick out.

The numbers are clearly painted on the opposite page, with corresponding pictures that you can use in counting games. The ideas will capture your child's imagination, and you'll enjoy reading them again.

Butterfly magic

Each number page is covered with the same number of butterflies for you to count up with your baby. Butterflies are wonderful creatures, because they are easy to draw, and you can use lots of different patterns and shapes on them.

- Draw the outline of a giant butterfly on a piece of paper. Decorate the butterfly together, using lots of different colours and patterns. Use this as an opportunity to introduce shapes to your child, so include lots of stars, triangles and circles on the wings. Count up the shapes and colours, and when you've finished, move on to a new butterfly.

Put on a play

- Use the book as inspiration for a short play. This is great if you have children of different ages. Ask older children to help you act out the numbers and the activities while the younger children watch and join in with actions and sounds.

- To make this even more fun, read the pages from the book in a different order, so that it becomes a guessing game. What's the number and what are they doing? Mime the actions and use props or costumes for effect.

- Once you have done this several times you can move on and make up new characters and actions for each number. So you might have *'Three clowns wearing gowns'*, or *'Five mice rolling dice'*.

Fun in the sun!

The book finishes with a lovely picture of everyone enjoying the sun.

- Use this as a starting point for your own picture entitled 'Enjoying the Sun'. Ask your child to help you come up with ideas for things you might include and why. Encourage him to think in terms of numbers, so he might draw three children, four dogs, five ice creams, six sandcastles and so on.

- Also think of different settings, for example, a garden or park like in the book, or a beach or playground. This is an opportunity to get really creative and also introduce lots of new vocabulary while you play!

29

Room on the Broom

by Julia Donaldson and Axel Sheffler (Macmillan Children's Books)

This wonderful rhyming tale is a delight to read. It rolls off the tongue with lots of lilting phrases and fun words that you will enjoy repeating. The story is about a kind witch who lets everyone ride on her broom. She stops to pick up various characters, but soon the broom gets so crowded that eventually it breaks. The story itself has a clever twist ending which sees the witch escape the clutches of a hungry dragon with the help of her new found friends. It is a great read at any time of day, but especially good for bedtime as it will leave your child feeling happy and satisfied.

Witch's spells

At the end of the story the witch makes a spell to create a brand new broomstick to carry everyone.

- Use this as inspiration for your own spells. Come up with a list of different spells. You might have 'Baby's spell for play time' or 'Baby's spell for eating her tea.' Think of all the different situations your baby encounters and create funny spells for them.

- Add a bit of drama by pretending you have a cauldron and you're adding things to it as you chant the rhyme.

For example:

'This spell is for baby's bedtime. It's to help her drift off to sleep and have lovely dreams. First we need a sprinkle of stardust and then a pinch of sugar because she's so sweet. Next we blow in a kiss, clap our hands three times and hey presto, the spell is complete!'

- Make this an enjoyable game and include your child. This works especially well in situations that your baby might find uncomfortable or different. For example, when you're taking her on a journey in the car and you want to calm her down and make it fun. By creating a spell, you're turning everything into an adventure.

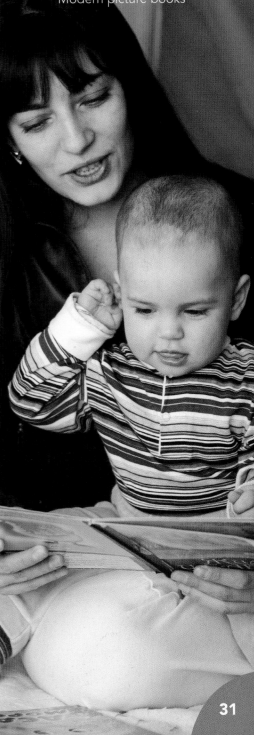

What makes a witch?

- Use the book as a starting point for creating a picture of a witch. Start by asking the question *'What makes a witch?'* and then help your child to come up with answers, like a pointy hat, a broom, a wand, a cauldron, a black cat and so on. Each time, repeat the question so that it becomes a game. Young children should find this quite easy because a witch is something they will have encountered in other stories.

- When you've come up with a list of things that make a witch, have fun drawing a picture together. Take this further by giving your witch a name and deciding whether she is good or bad. Where does she live and what does she enjoy doing?

- Your baby will enjoy helping to colour in the picture. An older child can get involved in the process of making up the witch and drawing some of the things you've mentioned.

- Have a go at making some of the items like the pointy hat or a magic wand. Talk about what each thing does, so for example, why does a witch need a wand? What does she use her cauldron for?

- When you've done this, experiment with other figures like kings, queens, dragons, magicians and so on. Repeat the process and create a picture together.

Safari Animals

by Paul Hess (Zero to Ten)

This is another beautiful book of verse in the *Animal Verse* series. *Safari Animals* will introduce your child to gorgeous landscapes and creatures. It uses colourful rhymes that you can enjoy repeating together.

Animal tales

- Use the book as a starting point for making up your own animal tales. Read the rhyme and then make up a story about the animals in the book. Alternatively, pick new animals and follow a similar format. Start with a poem, or a few repetitive phrases. To help ask yourself the following questions:

  - Where does the animal live?

  - What does it like doing?

  - What does it eat?

  - What does it look like?

  When you think of the animal what are the first words that come into your mind?

- Use easy rhyming sequences like those in the book. Remember this is for your baby so it doesn't have to be complicated. Think of words that go well together such as:

  - **Place** and **space**
  - **It** and **bit**
  - **Say** and **way**

  - **Here** and **there**
  - **Go** and **no**
  - **Play** and **day**

  - **To** and **do**

  Have a go at including some of these in your rhyme.

- If you've chosen one of the animals in the book, use the rhymes already given to help you come up with a story. For example, the Leopard ditty talks about the leopard not being the sort of cat that you should keep inside a flat. So what happens if you come home one day to find a leopard in your flat? What would happen next? Use this as a starting point for a short tale about how the leopard gets back to the jungle.

- Make some animal masks based on the characters in the book. This is a great activity for an older child. Get your child to pick an animal and draw the shape of its face on a piece of card. Decorate the mask using colours and paints.

- When they have finished have fun together pretending to be the different animals. Think about the way they move and the sounds they make.

- Swap masks and make this a game, where you each try to be a different animal.

- Talk about the characteristics of the animal: is it fast or slow, strong or weak? If you could be an animal which one would you choose to be and why?

The Foggy Foggy Forest

by Nick Sharratt (Walker Books)

This gorgeous book is a must for all parents and babies. With its see-through pages, and the opportunity to guess what the pictures are, it makes a great tool for storytelling and using the imagination. It also has some fun rhyming phrases and interesting words that you don't normally find in picture books. It is definitely one you'll keep coming back to time and time again!

Camera, action!

The book is written in a rhythmic question and answer format that is perfect for group storytelling. It's packed full of action phrases like 'a fairy queen on a trampoline' or 'a unicorn blowing a horn'.

- Use these phrases for making up actions and sounds. As you turn the pages to reveal 'What's in the foggy forest?' encourage your child to make up actions to go with each picture. Make sure you repeat each action in a sing-song fashion and go through it again, so that over time they begin to look out for words and anticipate what comes next.

- Ask an older child to have a go at drawing something else that might be lurking in the forest. Encourage her to think of actions to go with her pictures. For example, if she decides to draw a monkey, what would it be doing, eating a banana or swinging through the trees? Let her have fun with this, and come up with silly answers.

- Each time you read the book encourage your child to think of new ideas, so that you have lots of pictures and actions that you can add on at the end. This makes each storytelling experience unique!

Mirror mirror

- This is something you can do with groups of small children, or you can pair up with your child and have a go. You're going to pretend you're looking into a mirror. Think of a character that you might come across in the foggy forest, and then decide upon actions and sounds that your child can copy.

- Explain who or what you are, for example, *'Mummy's going to be a big bad wolf, she growls and snarls and pulls lots of funny faces.'* Experiment with sound and movement, and let your child come up with ideas that you can copy or help her develop.

What's in the tree?

- Get some black paper and, using chalk, draw a big tree with lots of branches. Add some shapes of animals, birds, children and flowers into the branches. Don't shade them in, just do the outline.

- Now ask your child what they think each shape is. Follow the format of the book by saying *'What could this be in the foggy foggy tree?'* To help, say *'Could it be... '* and insert what it is.

- Give your child lots of pointers and ask them questions such as *'What's it doing in the tree? ' 'Do you think it's having its tea?'* As they discover more about each mystery shape, let them decorate the picture using coloured paper, foil, glitter etc. You can use it as a wallchart, and add to it each reading session.

The Perfect Prince

by Paul Harrison and Sue Mason (Evans)

This picture book is excellent for all ages. The twist in the tale might be hard for very young children to understand, but the pictures will definitely capture their imagination and there's plenty of potential for games and rhymes. The story is loosely based on the fairy tale of *The Princess and the Frog*, but it has an altogether different and enchanting ending that will make you smile.

Prince Charming

In the story, Princess Isabella is being forced to choose a prince to marry. She meets many different princes in her search but none of them are right.

- Make up a rhyme about the different types of prince, using simple descriptive words. Make sure you use the colourful pictures to point out each type of prince and add in a few of your own, for example, a crooked prince or a grumpy prince, a bendy prince or a round one. So you might start with something like...

    'Here are a pack of princes, they come from all around. There's a quiet prince, and a scary prince and a prince who's very round. There's a tall prince and a short prince, a fat prince and a thin. A prince who likes to smile a lot and a prince who's very dim.'

- Put actions to the rhyme. So for the quiet prince you might place your finger in front of your mouth and go 'Sssshhhh'.

- Encourage your child to join in with the sounds and actions, and keep adding to it by using different types of prince, and simple actions and sounds. Finish the rhyme by asking about the perfect prince and what he might be like.

Frog fun!

The book turns the original fairy tale of *The Princess and the Frog* on its head, as the little princess eventually turns into the frog.

- What would it be like to be a frog? Where would you live and what would you eat? Who would be your friend? Ask your child to draw a picture of Isabella the frog in her new home. Help by suggesting some new friends and adventures that she could have.

- Have a go at making up some stories using Isabella as a starting point. Because she was once human she will be able to offer a different perspective to life on the pond. Get pictures of other pond creatures and use them to illustrate your tale.

The Real Story of Cinderella and the Ugly Sisters

by Liz Pichon (Little Tiger Press)

This book is bright, glitzy and lots of fun. It takes the traditional tale and turns it on its head. It uses colourful cats as the basis for the story, and includes lots of quirky additions and things you can pick out, as you read through. This is a book that you can return to again and again, and it's also a good starting point for further development and discussion as your child grows. Explore and enjoy this updated version of a classic!

Disco divas

There's a wonderful scene in the book where the Ugly Sisters, who are really good and kind, hit the dance floor at the Prince's ball.

- Recreate the scene, and put on some music. Pick a character for you and your baby and describe what you are doing, wearing and saying. Inject some movement into the story, and dance and sing. Clap your baby's hands and encourage them to move and sway. Babies love dancing and music, and there's no reason why you can't include this in the story.

- This is a great activity if you have a lot of children together. Re-tell the story until the point of the ball, and then get them to create the scene. Encourage them to get into character and dress up. This is all about having fun, and using the imagination!

Twist on the tale

- Just as Liz Pichon has transformed this classic tale and changed the bias, you can do the same with some of your favourite fairy tales. Stick to something simple, like reversing the characters so that good become evil. For example, in *The Three Little Pigs*, perhaps the pigs pick on the wolf and they won't let him in the house to play with them. What would happen next? Perhaps Mr Wolf falls down the chimney and the pigs get covered in soot and they all fall about laughing. The pigs see the error of their ways and decide that just because he's a wolf it doesn't mean that he's scary and so they all become friends.

- If your child is old enough, get her involved in creating the tale. This book includes lots of speech bubbles and comments from the characters which are fun to read out. Follow the same pattern and think about what Mr Wolf and the three pigs would say. Create catchy phrases that you can repeat together.

Lotions, potions, props and pans!

In the book, the two Ugly Sisters get ready for the ball by preening and using lots of magical lotions and potions especially for cats, like anti-pong spray and eau de cat.

- Think about other ideas for lotions and potions that they could use to make themselves look beautiful. Perhaps they could use spells to help.

- What else do they need to get to the ball? Point out some of the things in the book, and have a go at making up some props so that you can act the story out together. Drawing your child's attention to items and then helping her make connections with the real thing, is a great way to extend her vocabulary and understanding of language.

Toddle Waddle

by Julia Donaldson and Nick Sharratt (Macmillan Children's Books)

This is a wonderful book for babies and very young children. It is brightly coloured, with fabulous illustrations and lots of action on every page, the perfect picture book to capture young imaginations. Each page takes you on a journey, a child's day out, and all the amazing sounds he encounters. Great fun!

Stop and look

The first few pages of *Toddle Waddle* are like a train gathering speed. Each picture includes a new character, and also a new phrase to learn, until we eventually reach the page about half way through that says 'Stop!' At this point in the story, we see the characters gathered at a railing, mouths open, looking at something. What could they be looking at? What will be added to the next picture?

- Come up with ideas and encourage your child to have a go at drawing the next scene. What new characters will be there? Who could they be, and what will they be doing?

- This is the perfect springboard tale, because it reaches a point where the story could go anywhere. Ask an older child to pick a character, so for example they might choose the frog. What does the frog see? What happens next to him? Does he play with the boy and the dog? Perhaps he meets another frog, or maybe a little princess gives him a kiss and he turns into a prince?

- Encourage your child to come up with sounds to match their story ideas. If the frog jumps and lands in a puddle it might go 'Splish splosh' or 'Splott splatt'.

My favourite day out

- Ask a slightly older child to have a go at drawing and describing his perfect day out. Where would he go and who would he go with? What kinds of things would he do, and would he meet anyone there? What kind of actions and sounds would he experience?

- Encourage him to come up with pairs of rhyming words like the ones in *Toddle Waddle*. Help him make a touchy feely collage of his day, by including materials that remind him of how things feel and look.

- To help him stretch his imagination, ask him to make a collage about somewhere he has never been before, like space or fairyland. Encourage him to use everyday objects and materials to create his collage. For example, he might use tin foil for a space ship, or bottle tops for planets. This is great fun and it will get your child to use all his senses.

When a Monster is Born

by Sean Taylor and Nick Sharratt (Orchard)

This book is brilliant fun for parents and children. The story has lots of twists and turns with different options as to what the monster will do. The illustrations are bright and engaging and complement the wacky ideas.

The premise of the book is about what happens when a monster is born. According to the author, this is based on a traditional Brazilian poem about what happens when a baby is born. Each page takes you on the next step of its journey until eventually you come full circle to the point where the monster has its own baby and the whole process starts again.

Monster school

In the first few pages of this book, a monster is born and it lives under the bed. It then gets taken to school. At school it either sits quietly, does its homework or eats the headteacher!

- What would happen if you took a monster to school? Would it scare all the children, or would they make friends with it? Perhaps the monster would have its own school for little monsters?

- Encourage your child to have a go at creating a monster school. Start by asking her to draw a picture of the school and the monsters that go there. What kind of activities and games would they play?

- With an older child you can take this to the next level, by asking him to imagine he is a monster for the day. He has to report on what he has been doing. What did he learn in school? Who are his friends? What type of monster is he? Does he eat people?

Faraway forest

In the book the author mentions the Faraway Forest, which is where all the monsters live.

- With your child talk about what kind of a place this would be. Together come up with different words to describe the forest. If it helps draw a picture.

- Have a go at making up a poem (it doesn't have to rhyme) that tells a story. Put your child in the story as this will encourage her to join in. So you might say:

  'Molly went wandering one day on her own, to the Faraway Forest, where the monsters roam. She counted to three, one two three, then she yelled. "I'm lost and alone, I could do with some help."'

- Repeat this together, using the counting and shouting as points for your child to join in. Think about what might happen next. Ask her for ideas and together come up with the next couple of rhyming sentences. So you might say:

  'The bushes they rustled, the ground it shook. Molly was scared for she knew she was stuck. She could hear someone grumbling, his voice was so loud. "I'm a monster, I'm hungry!" He moaned and he growled.'

- Continue this pattern, coming up with a sentence or two then repeating that section until you are familiar with it, until you have created the poem together. Taking it step by step keeps it simple and fun and means you can add to it at any time.

Who's in the Loo?

by Jeanne Willis and Adrian Reynolds (Andersen)

This delightful picture book has all the ingredients that children love. It's colourful, easy to read, with lovely rhyming text, and it's also very silly! The premise of the book is who's in the loo? Each page offers up a different scenario from a school of skunks washing their tails, to a cat sailing a catamaran. The pictures are vibrant and there's plenty of detail to pick out. The funny ending will get you all laughing while reinforcing a good point, about washing hands.

Guess who?

- This book lends itself to a guessing game, as together you try and decide who's in the loo? Keep pausing as you read it, every few pages, to see if you can decide who it might be. Talk about the other animals and any that you might have forgotten.

- If your child is old enough, he might be able to offer suggestions of other animals and characters and what they might be doing in the toilet. What could possibly be taking all that time? Maybe it's a sloth sleeping, or a hippo ballet dancing! Be as creative as you like and have fun.

- This book is all about letting your imagination run riot. Encourage your child to do the actions that go with his suggestions, and while you're at it you could go through the book and think up actions and sounds to go with the other suggestions.

What rhymes with loo?

- This book is filled with rhyme, so make up your own toilet ditty. Take the word loo and together think of other words that rhyme with it. Make up a list. Now think of other things related to toilets. So you might have 'flush' or 'sit' or 'wash' and think of rhyming words to match them. So you might have flush, gush, mush, brush, push and so on, and sit, bit, hit, fit, pit, knit.

- Once you have come up with different groups of words it's time to put them together in a simple ditty. So you might start by saying:

Today I got locked in the loo,
With not very much to do.
I pushed the flush, watched the water gush.
Then jumped up and down 'Woo hoo!'

- Stick to this simple format and come up with more toilet ditties. If you have a group of children together you could run a competition for the best toilet rhyme, or sit them in the circle and go round the group making up rhymes together.

Roll reversal

- If you've got a surplus of loo roll, screw up little balls of it to make a collage. Ask your child to create a picture from the book, so they might want to copy something they've seen or do their own version. Using extra coloured paper, toilet roll, cotton wool and any other materials, stick on bits that you have to hand and turn it into a 3-D collage.

Classic
picture books

There are many wonderful pictures books that are considered classics of their time. They might have been around for a while, but they haven't lost any of their charm. The reason I have singled some of them out is because they have something special, staying power and the ability to connect with small children.

As adults we might ignore these books, thinking that they are old fashioned and not relevant, but they are still around for a reason. They made our hearts sing when we were little, and they are doing the same now for our children.

This chapter looks at some of these books. It shows you how you can make the best of them, how you can use them with your young child to help promote pre-reading skills, and most importantly, how you can both enjoy their timeless magic.

Don't be afraid to delve back into the past and pull out some of your favourites. Consider what you enjoyed as a child. What kinds of stories stick out in your mind? If they worked for you, they will work with your baby. This is not a comprehensive list. I have only scratched the surface with some of my personal favourites. So have fun. Enjoy and re-acquaint yourself with the gems of childhood.

Benjamin and the Box

by Alan Baker (Picture Lions)

This charming picture book was originally published in the 1970s but it is a story that is still popular today. It's about a hamster called Benjamin who finds a box marked 'Fragile'. Being a curious little hamster he's determined to find out what's inside and he tries everything to unlock it. Finally he manages to open the box and discovers a nice surprise. This is a gentle read with some interesting words and phrases.

What's in the box?

- Use the story as a straight forward guessing game. Show your child the box in the picture, and ask her to think about what might be inside. Come up with lots of ideas together and then ask her to draw a picture of what she thinks is inside the box before you carry on with the story.

- Take this a step further by creating your own magical box just like Benjamin's. Decorate a shoe box. Every week put something different in the box and encourage your child to guess what could be inside. Choose interesting objects that you can talk about. For example, something that you use in the kitchen.

- Alternatively put a different word in the box every day. This could be your magic word of the day. Encourage your child to use it as much as possible by giving her a gold star every time she puts it in a sentence!

Benjamin's tool box

Benjamin uses a range of tools and techniques to open the box.

- Go through each one and talk about how it works. Together, come up with sounds and words associated with that particular tool and add it in to the story. So with the hammer you might say *'He banged and he smashed, he thwacked and he thumped!'*

- Do the actions to go with each tool. Are there any more things that Benjamin could have used to open the box? What else could he have done? See if you can come up with other ideas, and have fun extending the story.

Hamster fun!

- Use the story as a starting point for looking at hamsters and other pets. Encourage your child to have a go at making up a day in the life of a hamster. Where does he live? What does he like doing? Does he have any hamster friends? What other animals might be friends with your hamster?

- Use soft toys and make up a play about what the animals get up to. If you don't have any toy animals that you can use, invest in some finger puppets, or use old socks for the different animals. Go through all the different types of small animals that you might have as pets and include them all. This is lots of fun and an entertaining game you can play with groups of children.

Dry Bones

illustrated by Kate Edmunds (Child's Play Classic Books with Holes series)

Based on the traditional African American spiritual rhyme, this lovely book will help small children learn about different parts of the body. The illustrations are fun, and the holes on each page make the learning interactive. There's also a full skeleton at the back of the book, which lists scientific names for all the main bones in the body. Once your child has got into the swing of the rhyme, you can turn to the back of the book and use the skeleton as a learning tool.

Body talk

As each part of the body is mentioned, we see a lovely illustration of the skeleton using that part of the body in an activity.

- Go through each one, and ask your child to think about other activities that you could do that use that part of the body. Together come up with a list of different actions and movements. For example, on the first page it says *'The toe bone's connected to the foot bone. The foot bone's connected to the ankle bone,'* and we have a picture of the two skeletons playing football. Your list might include: we walk, tap, dance, paddle, jump, hop, skip and so on.

- Add a new dimension to the rhyme by going through each sentence as above, and then adding on what we can do with each bone. So you might say *'And with our feet and ankles, we walk, we skip, we hop, we dip. We paddle, we jump, we splash, we stump!'* Repeat over and over, and create a rhythm, picking up speed each time you do it, and adding in actions.

Skeleton tales

- Imagine you live in a ghostly world full of skeletons just like those in the book. What would this place be like, and would other creatures live there? Use this as the starting point for a story about a skeleton boy, who lives in the land of bones.

- Help your child to draw a picture of this world, and think about the types of characters that might live there. What would the skeleton boy be like? Perhaps he's a just a normal boy who wants to play, and have fun, but he doesn't have anyone to play with? What happens next?

What dem bones gonna do?

Towards the end of the book, we come to the chant 'Dem bones, dem bones gonna walk around.'

- Use this in a simple game with groups of children. Start by reading the book and when you reach this point, ask the children to join in and do whatever it says the bones do, so you could say 'Dem bones, dem bones, gonna jump and clap,' or 'dance around' or 'wiggle and shake'. Encourage the children to take it in turns to call out different suggestions.

51

I am the Music Man

illustrated by Debra Potter
(Child's Play Classic Books with Holes series)

This is a brilliant adaptation of the popular nursery song. The cut-out pictures really bring the tale to life. Young children can peer into each window and discover who is playing what, and at the end there are lots of instruments to learn about. Sit your baby on your lap and either read the book, or sing it. Use the colourful images to ask questions about all the different characters and what they are playing.

What does it sound like?

- There are so many different types of instruments in this book, it can be quite confusing for young children. Help your child to understand by giving them samples of what each one might sound like. So a piano might go 'tinkle tinkle tinkle,' and a bass drum might go 'boom boom boom.' Keep it simple, and change your voice and expression with each one. Encourage your child to join in.

- Very young babies won't understand the context of the song, but they will enjoy the interaction. So encourage them to burble, babble and make lots of noise!

Animal magic

The clever illustrations mean there's so much to see and talk about as you go through this book.

- Point out the animals on each page and discuss what they are doing.

- Take each of the animals in turn and think about the sounds they make and what instrument might suit them. So you might have a mouse playing a flute, or a dog on the guitar. Together create your own animal band, using all the creatures in the book and giving them instruments to play.

- Draw pictures of each one, and make up a rhyme or song for them. For example, 'I am the music man and in my band I have: a mouse with a flute going toot toot toot, and a cat clashing symbols, all ratty tat tat!' Think of as many combinations as you can, and using the pictures that your child has created, go through your new song, putting in sounds and actions.

- This works particularly well if you're trying to keep a group of children occupied because each one takes responsibility for a different character and sound. Go through the rhyme together, acting it out, and let each child have a go at pretending to be a character.

Music master

- You don't have to have real instruments to make up a band! Encourage your child to create his own instruments using everyday items from around the home. Try filling an empty container with dried beans to make a maraca, or use the lid from a tin of sweets as a symbol. Even shaking card, or tapping on the table top makes a noise that can become part of the percussion.

- When you have enough instruments together, encourage your child to have a go at becoming a one-man band and make some noise!

Orange Pear Apple Bear

by Emily Gravett (Macmillan Children's Books)

This is a lovely book for babies, and you can use it from day one. It's simple, rhythmic and beautifully illustrated. Emily Gravett has picked four words that go perfectly together and work in so many different ways. It's a joy to read to babies, and will soothe them into sleep. The repetition helps them make sense of the words, and the pictures are fun and easy to understand.

Colour combinations

In the book the author has put different combinations of the words together. See how many you can come up with and encourage your child to have a go at drawing them. You might have a bear pear, and an orange apple, or vice versa. Add in new words to the mix to keep this fresh, so how about 'honey' and 'bunny'. The two words rhyme and would fit into the pattern. You could have honey bear, and orange bunny, or bunny honey, and orange bear. If your child is old enough encourage him to come up with other fruits and animals that you could add to the story.

- Together can you come up with rhymes and pictures to illustrate this? You might include a cat and a blackberry, a dog and a cherry, or a mouse and a plum. Make a list of all the animals and fruits you can introduce into the story and fit them together so they make a rhyme e.g. banana llama or strawberry teddy.

- Try swapping colour combinations around, so imagine if you had an orange pear, or a red orange, or a bear that looks like a red orange? Don't be afraid to experiment. This is a great way to come up with unique characters and ideas for future stories and rhymes.

Potty picture cards

- Make picture cards that you can use in a simple descriptive game. Choose some of the ideas in the book and think of your own different coloured fruit. Be adventurous and go for wacky things like blue spotted bananas and hairy apples. Draw the pictures on the card and include key words like 'spotty', 'blue' and 'banana'. Share the cards with your child and take it in turns to read and describe the picture you have.

- Alternatively, play a guessing game where you try to discover what type of fruit the other player has by asking yes/no questions.

- To extend this, make up poems to go with the picture card you have selected. Use the key words as a starting point and together think about rhyming words and other adjectives to describe the picture until you have enough to make up a short ditty. This activity works well as a party game, as it's something that the children can work on together in groups or pairs. Encourage them to think of actions to go with the poem, and then allow them time to share with the rest of the children!

Owl Babies

by Martin Waddell (Walker Books Ltd)

This gorgeous picture book is loved by parents and children. It's a simple tale about three owl babies who wake up one night to find that their Mum has flown the nest. The tale shows them venturing further afield in search of their Mum, and talking about where she might be. Eventually she returns and they all celebrate. The story touches brilliantly on the theme of independence, as there's a sense of the owl babies coming to terms with the situation and dealing with their fear of abandonment.

What next?

- Play the 'What happens next?' game with this book. When you get to the point where the babies wake up and discover their Mum has gone, pause and ask *'What happens next?' Where could Mummy be? What could she be doing?'* Also ask what the babies should do? Should they stay put in their nest or venture out to find her?

Three owls in a nest

- Help your child to make their own owls' nest. Take a shoe box and imagine that it's the hollow in a tree. What kind of things would be in there? Use scrunched-up paper, feathers, cotton wool, and bits of cloth to create the perfect owls' nest. Stick cotton wool together to make each of the little owls. Give them names and put them in the nest.

- Now make up a simple rhyme that you can chant together. Something like:

  'Three little owls in the nest, one called Sally, one called Pete, and one called Fred with really big feet!'

- Count out the owls and pick them up. Place them in and out of the nest, so, for example, there might be two birds in the nest and one outside. Encourage your child to have a go at counting how many birds are outside the nest and how many birds are inside. Add in different types of birds, and increase the numbers. This makes an enjoyable interactive counting game.

Magic masks

- This activity is great for an older child. Have a go at making magic owl masks. The secret with these masks is that when you put them on, you become an owl! Start by cutting out card in the shape of an owl's head. Remember to include pointed ears and two large holes for owlish eyes.

- Encourage your child to decorate the mask using coloured pens, crayons, paints and so on. Suggest that she collects feathers from the garden or park to stick on the mask.

- When you've finished, take it in turns to wear the mask and become an owl. What sort of noise does an owl make? How does it fly? Go outside and let your child have fun pretending to be an owl.

- Make this the starting point for some owl storytelling. Discuss why owls are different from the other birds that you might find in the garden.

Spot Bakes a Cake

by Eric Hill (Warne)

This lift-the-flap book is simple, colourful and lots of fun. Babies will love being able to touch the pages and uncover the hidden pictures. The story is straight forward and enjoyable to read, but most importantly it offers plenty of scope for you to come up with related activities and have fun together. The story is about Spot the dog who wants to bake a cake for his Dad's birthday. He gets a little help from Mum and also the friendly mouse. We see the cake at every stage throughout the book until eventually Spot proudly presents it to his Dad.

Bake a cake

- This book is the perfect introduction to baking a cake. When your child is young, every day includes lots of new experiences and baking a cake is one of them. It's an excuse to get messy and have fun, but also for them to learn about the process of creating something.

- Use the act of making a cake, identifying and collecting all the ingredients, mixing them up and then waiting for them to cook as an introduction to writing a story. It is the same thing. We collect the characters, the setting and the adventure and we put them all together and mix it up. When we're finished we have an exciting new story to share!

- If you don't actually want to bake a cake, then just talk about it. Come up with ideas for the ingredients together, make a list, or draw them, and instead of baking the real thing, create a cake using a cardboard box. Decorate it with coloured paper, paints, glitter, and cotton wool.

- Decide what type of cake it will be and what it might taste like. Who are you making the cake for? Perhaps your cake might be a magic one for the fairies? If so, what kind of ingredients will you use? Make up a story as you go along and enjoy your cake-making experience!

Party patterns

In the book Spot has a go at icing his Dad's cake. He comes up with lots of different patterns.

- Explore patterns and shapes with your child. Create a book of cake-making decorations, and start with simple shapes like circles and squares. Trace them on the paper and then encourage your child to colour them in, or follow the lines and if they're old enough have a go at copying your drawing. With babies just trailing their finger around the shape and making up a simple repetitive rhyme will help them develop key pre-reading skills.

- As you progress through the book introduce different patterns. Use star shapes and flowers and connect them up. Encourage your child to do the same using letters and joining them together, so that you have pages of patterns.

- Your child can decorate the patterns using crayons and glitter. The idea is to make the book as colourful as possible, while helping your child learn about shapes and how they work together to form patterns, pictures and writing.

The Gruffalo

by Julia Donaldson and Axel Scheffler (Macmillan Children's Books)

This much-loved book has become a classic because of its creative subject matter, the twists and turns of the tale, and the lovely rhyming prose. The story is about a clever mouse who manages to trick all of his predators into not eating him by using a made-up monster called the Gruffalo. The surprise twist is that the Gruffalo really does exist and is intent on having the mouse for tea, but again he uses his wits to outsmart the monster and scare him away.

The story packs a powerful message, that it doesn't matter how small you are, you can overcome the biggest scariest monster by using your brain! This is a great lesson to explore with small children.

Making up noises

- As you go through the book have a go at making up noises for each character. So every time you mention the mouse make a squeaking noise and encourage your child to join in. With the fox you might make a yapping yelping noise, with the owl a hooting sound and with the snake a wonderful hissing sound. Finally when it comes to the Gruffalo make up a noise that you think the monster might make, perhaps a gruffing huffing noise?

- Sound effects will add depth and colour to the story and help your baby understand what is going on, and a little about each animal. She might even try to join in. If your baby starts to move, gurgle or chatter in any way it's because she is having fun and connecting to the tale!

Gruffalo number fun

- Use the big picture of the Gruffalo in a fun counting game. Start with something simple, so you might ask *'How many horns does a Gruffalo have?'* and then count them together. Use your baby's fingers on the page to point things out. With an older child use your fingers to count together.

- Then you might say, *'How many tusks does a Gruffalo have?'* Ask the same questions about teeth, ears, eyes, nails, tails, prickles on his furry back and so on. There are lots of things to notice about the picture and some lovely descriptions in the book, so use these to make this an entertaining activity.

Monster magic

- A slightly older child will really enjoy making up her own monster. Talk about what the monster will look like, will it be large or small? Will it have horns, three heads and so on? What will she call it? Think of interesting words that she can use to make up a name.

- Once she has done this, have a go at making up a story where her new monster meets the Gruffalo. What happens next? Do they become friends? It might be a very lonely life for a monster in the wood. Perhaps the new monster also scares the Gruffalo away and becomes friends with the mouse?

- If you have a group of children, encourage them to act out the story, each taking it in turns to be the Gruffalo, the mouse, or a monster of their choice.

The Very Busy Spider

by Eric Carle (Puffin)

This is an Eric Carle classic and a lovely board book that babies will respond well to. The story is about a spider who is so engrossed in making her web that nothing distracts her. Various animals come along and ask the spider to do things with them, but the spider is too busy making her web to join in. In the end she has made the most beautiful web, but after all that work she's very tired and falls asleep.

The book has an added dimension in that it's touchy feely. If you place your fingers over the web you can feel it taking shape. Children will love this almost 3-D effect to the story.

Animal sounds

The book introduces lots of animals and the sounds they make.

- Go through the book pointing out the different animals and the sounds they make. Encourage your baby or toddler to join in with you. When you've covered all the animals in the story, introduce some new ones. For example, you might have a cuckoo, or a snake or a lion. Don't be afraid to use different types of animals, and think about words associated with them. You might say that the slithery snake slides along the grass, and goes *'Hiss hiss!'* or a giant bear strides through the wood and goes *'Grrrrrrrrrrrrrr who's there?'*

- Take this a step further by having the spider respond so that you're adding to the tale. Repeat all the different animals and their sounds, and then return to the tale and say that nothing and no-one could distract the little spider from her work.

Web magic

- Together you're going to create some magical spider's webs. Draw a pattern with some glue on a piece of black card. Encourage your child to join in and get creative using circles, stars and any shapes that she already knows. Sprinkle glitter over the design. Shake it on to the card and then get rid of any excess glitter. Add sequins for more effect.

- Once you've created your web make a spider for it. Draw a picture based on the illustrations in the book or make one using cotton wool dipped in black paint and then add pipe cleaners for legs.

- Use this as the starting point for a new story about the spider. Give her a name and talk about where she lives. Does she have a family? Give them names too and talk about what they might do. Do her children go to spider school and what kind of things do they learn there, web making and weaving or how to catch flies?

- Give her a character by adding in some quirky details, perhaps she wears wellington boots on her feet when it rains, or has a bow tie or a hat? By adding in amusing details you're helping your child to build up a picture of the character which will form the springboard for lots of new tales.

The Very Hungry Caterpillar

by Eric Carle (Puffin)

This all time classic is a favourite with all age groups. It's a lovely gentle tale about a caterpillar who manages to munch his way through lots of different types of food. Eventually he builds a cocoon and turns into a beautiful butterfly.

The book is very tactile with holes in the pages where the caterpillar has munched. This is perfect for little fingers to explore and have fun with. The story is a simple introduction to the wonders of nature and a great starting point for further adventures outside.

Count the caterpillar

In the book the caterpillar eats through two pears, three plums and so on, building up the number of different types of fruit.

- Use these pages to improve your child's numeracy by mixing up the order. Go to the strawberries first and see if he can count with you the number of strawberries with holes in. Then go back to the plums and forwards to the oranges. Then count the number of holes in the leaf together. This is a quick fire game that you can play with more than one child – the idea is that they have to shout out the number of items on the page. Let them take it in turns to flip the pages.

- Take the game outside by encouraging your child to see if he can spot any caterpillars in the garden or park. Talk about other insects that you might find outside and make a list, including ladybirds, beetles, ants, flies, bees, butterflies, wasps, caterpillars, slugs, worms and so on. Together add up how many you see.

- Create a colourful picture chart which you can add to every day. Get your child to help you draw a picture of an insect, and then leave a space so they can mark in how many they see over time.

- Conduct a mini survey of all the creatures you can find in your garden or park over the summer months.

Butterfly fingers

- Get messy and use paint pots and finger tips to create some symmetrical patterns. Fold a piece of paper in half and draw a wing on one side. Get your baby to dab their fingers in different coloured paint and create a pattern on the wing. Now fold the paper over, press together and watch as the full butterfly image emerges.

- Cut the butterflies out and hang them from the ceiling above your baby's bed. They are now in the ideal position to incorporate into a spot of bedtime storytelling. Give each butterfly a name and make up a story about where they come from. Perhaps they live in fairyland, or in sleepy world where they flutter over the heads of all the sleeping children and give them sweet dreams?

Three Wise Old Women

by Elizabeth T Corbett and Yu-Mei Han (Dutton Children's Books)

This delightful book is based on an old fashioned nonsense rhyme written in the late 1800s about three wise old women. The story tells how they go on an adventure and manage to get themselves lost. The book is beautifully illustrated, with vibrant expressive pictures that your child will love. The tale itself allows plenty of opportunities for storytelling games, and its wacky nature means you'll have lots of fun reading it.

What's the ladder?

In the book the women take a ladder with them as they begin their journey. The ladder soon becomes essential to their plans as they use it to escape bears and sail the sea.

- What other things could a ladder be used for? Encourage your child to come up with ideas. Perhaps they could use the ladder to leapfrog over trees? Or maybe they could use it to slide down mountains? Together, add new escapades to their journey by drawing colourful pictures of the ladder in use.

- Take this to the next stage by making up a new story about a magical ladder. Put your child in the story, by suggesting that one day she goes to the park and finds an enormous ladder reaching up to the sky. What happens next? Does she climb the ladder? Where does it lead to? Perhaps it takes her to a new world, or maybe she's high up in the clouds. What can she see? This type of story is great for stimulating the imagination.

Wise women at play!

As you turn the first page you'll see a wonderful picture of the three women on the farm.

- The artist has put so much into this picture that it makes the ideal basis for an easy storytelling game. Start by pointing out the women and describing what they are doing, but do this as if you are telling a story. You might say:

  'One day there were three wise old women and they were working on the farm. The first one was washing the pigs, the second was feeding sausages to the dog and the third was trying to catch the cockerel.'

- Now go into more detail, pick out the other animals in the picture, and talk about their antics. If your child is old enough, ask her to pick things out, and encourage her to think about what might happen next. Perhaps the old woman leans too far out of the window and lands on top of the cow, who in fright goes speeding off into the distance. Have fun coming up with other storylines.

Springboard tale

The book finishes on a cliff-hanger. What happens next to the old women? Do they ever make it home? Nobody knows.

- Use this as a springboard to a new adventure. Where do you think the old women sailed to on the ladder?

- Make your own ladder boat by placing two chairs together. You and your child can sit on the boat and imagine where you could sail to and what adventures you might have! Have fun and pretend to row on the sea.

We're Going on a Bear Hunt

by Michael Rosen and Helen Oxenbury (Walker Books Ltd)

This winner of the Smarties book prize is a comic masterpiece. It is fun to read and a real adventure story that your baby can get involved in. The pictures add much to the description and the clever use of language really adds to the pace of the book.

The story is about a family who decide to go on a bear hunt and they encounter lots of different things along the way from snow storms to deep dark woods. Eventually they really do find a bear, who is not too happy to be disturbed. The bear hunt soon becomes a bear chase as they race all the way back home to hide under the bed covers!

Obstacle and action

With each page the children come across a new obstacle on their journey. It could be mud, or a river or long grass.

- When you reach the obstacle in the book, talk about how the children might get through it. Include the descriptive sounds in the book and come up with some of your own. So, for example, you might read that the long grass was 'swishy swashy,' and then think about other pairs of words to describe it, such as 'scritchy scratchy' or 'wishy washy!'

- Talk about how the children would move through the grass. Would they take giant strides and wade, or would it be so long that they'd have to use their hands to pull the blades apart? What could be hiding in the grass? Maybe they could find something in the grass that might help them in their adventures!

- Perhaps the children meet other interesting animals along the way. Come up with an alternative story, where lots of other creatures join in the bear hunt!

What happens next?

The book ends with the children hiding under the bed clothes, and the bear waiting outside.

- With your child talk about what might happen if they opened the door? Would it be a friendly bear? Perhaps the bear is so lonely that he only wanted to play with the children.

- Come up with a new story with the bear as the focus. Encourage your child to get involved and think of ideas. What would the bear and the children do next? What kinds of games might they play? Ask your child to draw a picture that shows a different ending to the book.

Act it out

- Go on a real bear hunt around the garden or park! This is a lovely idea if you're having a party and need a fun game to entertain the children. Hide two or three teddy bears outside, and ask the children to find them. You could include pictures of bears too. The children get points for every bear they find, so the child with the most points wins the hunt. Encourage the children to chant the words from the book as they go along.

- Reverse the game by asking one child to become the bear, and the rest of the children to hide. The child who is the bear must hunt down the children. Encourage them to act the part, and pretend to be a bear, by stamping and growling and sniffing!

The Tiger Who Came to Tea

by Judith Kerr (Collins Picture Lions)

This multi-million selling picture book is still a hit with children today. Its timeless sense of fun, engaging pictures, and simple storyline make it suitable for babies and young children. Sophie and her Mummy are just about to sit down to tea when the doorbell rings. They wonder who it can be, so they open the door and find a very hungry tiger standing there. He politely asks if he can join them for tea, so they say yes.

The story then continues with the Tiger eating everything that they give him, and more. He eats so much that he eats all the food in the cupboards and drinks all the water from the taps. Then when he's had his fill, he thanks them and leaves. The problem is that there's nothing to eat or drink in the house. So when Daddy comes home they all decide to go out for dinner. The next day Sophie makes sure that they buy a very large tin of tiger food, in case he comes to visit again!

Tiger's tea party

- Get your child to imagine that they're throwing a tea party for Tiger's birthday. What kinds of food are they going to include? Get into the spirit of it by baking some cakes together. Invest in some plain paper plates and ask your child to decorate them with drawings and patterns that Tiger might like. How would he decorate the table? Tape squares of paper together to make a large tablecloth and encourage your child to experiment with glitter, glue, tinsel, and paints.

- Next ask him to think about the kind of games he would like to play. Perhaps pass the parcel, or hide and seek? Perhaps he would like to take it in turns to ride the tiger?

- Finally, ask your child to think about other animal guests. Perhaps he would also invite Bear and Monkey. Make up a fantasy guest list of creatures for the perfect tea party. If you have a large group of children you can get them to act out different parts. Help them to create animal masks or pictures. Place the masks on the seats around the table. Put on some fun party music and get the children to run around the table. When the music stops they have to grab a seat and put on the mask. They then have to pretend to be that animal for a few minutes until the music starts up again.

Tiger tins

We all know that tiger food in a tin doesn't exist, but if it did, what would the tin look like? Ask an older child to come up with a design for the packaging. It might be a picture of a tiger, or it might be a picture of all the types of food that they like to eat. Go back to the book for inspiration and use some of the things that Tiger eats as suggestions for pictures.

Mog the Forgetful Cat

by Judith Kerr (HarperCollins Children's Books)

This charming picture book is a timeless classic. The engaging tale and beautiful illustrations make it a pleasure to read and share with children. The story itself is about a cat called Mog, who is very forgetful. She forgets that she's eaten, she forgets what she's doing, and most importantly she forgets that she has a cat flap so that she can get back into the house. This causes huge problems and means that poor Mog starts to get on everyone's nerves jumping up at the window to get in and causing all sorts of accidents.

Eventually she ends up out in the cold and dark and feeling very sorry for herself. But that's when the story takes a turn for the better, because Mog sees an unwanted visitor in the house, and jumps up at the window thinking he'll let her in. He turns out to be a burglar, and the noise she makes wakes everyone up. So Mog saves the day, the burglar is caught, and she gets a special medal for her bravery! Who could fail to love a cat like Mog?

Forget me not

- Together with your child think of all the things you do throughout the day that could be forgotten. So, for example, having a wash, brushing teeth, eating breakfast, getting dressed, feeding the cat.

- Next create a 'forget me not' poster of your child's daily routine. So for each activity ask your child to draw a little picture. When she's finished think of key words to do with the activity. For example, brushing teeth might include scrubbing, brushing, rinsing.

- Finally write a sentence beneath each picture to describe what your child is doing. So you might say 'At the start of the day I brush my teeth.'
  Then for the next picture, 'Next I wash my face'. Try to use some of the descriptive words that you talked about earlier. So you might say 'I splash and pat, and rub it dry.'

- Go through the poster together reading the sentences and describing each activity.

Mog's adventures

- What would happen if Mog left the house, and walked through the garden gate? She might find herself on the street, and what would happen if she forgot how to get home? This is possible as Mog is such a forgetful cat! Make this the start of a new 'Mog' story. Begin by saying:

  'One day Mog decides to go for a walk. The sun is out and she finds herself on the street. She decides to follow Debbie on her way to school, only she forgets where she is, and how to get home.'

- Ask your child to draw a picture of what happens next. Where does she go and how does she find her way home? If it helps, come up with some ideas. For example, what if Mog follows Debbie all the way into school? She might visit different classes. She might join in a game of netball, or eat the cakes they bake in cookery. She might hop on the map in geography, or decide to join in a drama class and make the teacher jump. There are so many things that Mog could get up to, and then to solve the problem of how she gets home, she might climb inside Debbie's school bag.

- Alternatively, Mog might end up at the shops. So she might steal sausages from the butcher, or get covered in flour at the bakers. She might come home in a shopping trolley. Talk about different variations, and encourage your child to come up with two or three different endings and pictures.

Where the Wild Things Are

by Maurice Sendak (Red Fox)

This is probably one of the most famous picture books of all time. This hauntingly beautiful story was first published in 1963 and it is still a favourite today. The story is about Max, a naughty young boy who sails away to the land where the Wild Things live. The monsters try and scare him, but Max proves he's far wilder than they could ever be, and in the end they make him their King. But Max misses home and decides to leave them. He returns in his little boat across the sea to find supper waiting for him.

There are some fabulous illustrations in this book, and the pictures alone tell a beautiful tale of how one boy learns an important lesson about love, friendship, and behaving himself!

Enchanted forest

The adventure begins when a forest begins to grow in Max's bedroom over night.

- Use this as inspiration to create an enchanted forest for your child. Choose a corner of his bedroom and talk about what kinds of things you might find in a magical forest. If you don't want to decorate the walls, make large posters of trees. Draw the outline of the shapes on large sheets of paper by copying the trees from the book. Make them big and encourage your child to colour or paint them.

- Use empty kitchen rolls taped together for trunks. Perch old lamp shades on top, or if you prefer cut out paper leaves and glue them on at angles. Invest in a green rug to represent the grass, or just use old scarves and pieces of fabric. Make this a real adventure and get your child to create a sea, by painting large squares of paper blue. Finally take an old cushion or a cardboard box to use as a boat.

- When everything is ready use this setting as a platform for some storytelling. Your child is going to follow in Max's footsteps. He sails in the boat to reach the enchanted forest where the wild things live. What happens next? Does he see a monster? Perhaps they make him king too. You can use an old hat, or create a cardboard crown and decorate it with buttons, glitter and ribbons.

- Once he's king ask him to make up some rules. Perhaps he decides that everyone must eat chocolate in his land or everyone must smile? You could make a chant for the king to repeat, or a rhyme. Enjoy play acting together, and turn your ready made forest into a place of wonder and magic!

Make a monster outfit

In the story Max looks like a monster thanks to his pyjamas.

- Help your child get into the spirit of the book by making him look like a monster too. Find an old playsuit, and customise it. Add on a tail using cotton wool, or bits of string. Make a monster hat with horns using rolled-up paper. Make some floppy monster ears using old scraps of fabric.

- Ask your child what he thinks a monster might look like. Encourage him to make monster sounds and to think about how he should move.

Choosing
and using
picture books

I hope that this book is giving you lots of ideas on how to use your favourite picture books, as well as getting the most out of new books. This is something that anyone can do, and with almost any picture book. It's about picking the right story and looking out for key points that you can use. In this section we'll look at these triggers, and offer suggestions to get you started. Once you get into the habit of looking at books this way, you'll see the potential in almost everything. Picture books are written in a style that will appeal to young minds. All the ingredients are there; it's about using them in a variety of ways to stretch the imagination.

Start by thinking about how you choose a book for your baby. What is the first thing that you look out for? Obviously the cover has to be eye-catching, and if it is, then you're guaranteed that there will be plenty of lovely illustrations to explore and talk about together. Also look at the title, is it snappy and fun? If it comes in the form of a question, then you know that it will be answered in the pages of the book, so there are going to be opportunities to delve into the subject and take it further. This chapter shows what else you should look out for.

Touchy feely tales

Babies love the opportunity to touch books. It's their way of reaching out to the world and making sense of it. They like to poke and prod and tap and pull. Look for books that are hard wearing but also have lots of pull-out, pop-up bits.

Books might be made of cloth, or have bits of fabric used to build up a collage. Again this will encourage your baby to handle the book, and from this he will learn the mechanics of reading, of holding the book the right way up and turning the pages in the correct order.

What's the story?

Consider what the book is about. Does it have a story? Lots of picture books concentrate on one subject area, offering pictures and words to introduce new vocabulary. Some have more story than others. There is nothing wrong with either type of book, it just depends what you want to get out of it.

Go for a balance of both. Try to pick simple tales with an interesting message. Look at the subject matter, is it stimulating and fun? For example, if the book is about living on a farm, there will be plenty of opportunity to use farm sounds and actions, but if the book is about the classroom then you won't have the same potential for storytelling. However, you might find other things you can use to come up with interesting activities and games.

In the early stages it's a good idea to pick books that include experiences that will be familiar to your baby, but as he gets older don't be afraid to explore other areas. Books about

things he hasn't encountered can be incredibly rewarding, and great starting points for learning.

Go with your initial reaction. If it looks like it's going to be an engaging read, go for it!

Words and pictures

Now look at the actual words and pictures. How are they spaced on the page? Are they the right size and shape, and are they written in an interesting way? For example, perhaps they are written in the form of a shape or a swirling pattern across the page. You can use this when you're telling the story, and help your baby make the shapes with his fingers.

Next, look at the pictures. Do they capture what is being said? If you didn't have the words there, would you be able to tell what was happening in the story? Pictures paint a thousand words and you can use them to encourage your child to come up with his own ideas.

Repetition and rhyme

Go for books that include lots of repetition. Look out for key words or phrases that are repeated often. Babies and small children respond well to this, it gives them something to look out for and helps them get to grips with language. If the book doesn't include repetition you can always make this up yourself, if there's a word or two that you think stands out.

Rhyme is also important, so look out for stories told in verse, or text that has some kind of rhythmic flow to it. It doesn't have to rhyme completely, but if it has some kind of pattern it will make it easier for your child to follow and it will also give you something to focus on and use in a related activity.

Hints, tips and tools

Now you have the book you can start by looking out for things you can use. Here are some tried and tested tips.

Springboard stories

In every story there is a point of crisis. This is where the story can go in any direction. Sometimes the point of crisis is a major problem that needs to be resolved, and sometimes it's just a springboard where the story turns into an adventure and the character takes a step off the path into the woods. Think of this point as a plateau from which you can take the tale anywhere.

- If your child is old enough you can use this by asking them to get involved. What do they think will happen next? Encourage them to draw a picture and come up with a different ending. Perhaps they want to have a go at acting it out?

- The beauty of a springboard story is that it can take you anywhere and from that one single point you can come up with a number of different tales and activities.

Character types

Does the book have lots of unusual characters in it? Perhaps it has different types of wizards or monsters.

- If this is the case use it to come up with other characters in the same genre. Ask your child to create their own monster and give it a name. Ask them questions and encourage them to create a back story for their character.

- Take this a step further by taking the new character and either put it in the book, or create a new tale for it together.

Magic words

- Decide upon a magic word for the book. Pick something unusual, and if possible something that occurs more than once. Tell your child that they have to look out for the magic word. If they hear it or see it, they must shout it out three times.

- If your child is old enough, introduce a magic word for the week. Pick something that is likely to appear in the books you read together. Stick the word about the house, and use it at every opportunity. Your child gets a gold star or a prize for every time they use the word in a sentence.

Riddle and rhyme

- Look out for words that sound good, and also rhyming words and phrases that go together. Use this as a starting point for collecting more words that sound interesting or fit in pairs. Try to stick to the subject matter, so if the story is about a train clattering down the track, stick to words that describe the sound and movement of the train. By doing this you are increasing your child's range of vocabulary and helping them discover how words and sounds fit together.

Copy cat!

- Are there any activities in the book that you can copy with your baby? For example, if the child makes some biscuits, perhaps you can do the same thing and point out the similarities as you go along. If the story is about a trip to the seaside, use this to remind your child of the time you went to the seaside.

- Books are great starter activities for introducing something more practical. Look out for tales that include things you want your baby to learn, for example, potty training.

Story-building

This is something you can start when your baby is born, and continue while she's in her pre-school years. Every time you tell your baby a story, you're sharing a very special experience. You're introducing her to new words and helping her make sense of the world.

Take note

- Make a record of each tale. This is particularly useful if you are making up your own stories. It's a great way to see what you've done, and how your storytelling skills are developing. When your baby gets older she will be able to share in the creative journey and remember some of the lovely tales you told together.

- Either begin a story journal and write down snippets of the tale or if you have space and the artistic inclination, make a story tree or noticeboard. Start at the bottom as if you're working from the roots upwards and attach pictures, key words and phrases that were a part of the story. Add in other things that were symbolic. So, for example, if the story was about bedtime, you might want to glue on some silver stars. Have fun with this, and as your child grows she will be able to join in and decorate the tree with you.

- You will be able to go back to some of your earlier tales and use what you have done as inspiration for either expanding them, or coming up with something new. Your child will also be able to use this as a tool for storytelling.

Storytelling Space

- Take this a step further and dedicate a corner of your baby's room for this type of activity. Have a go at building a story wall, and decorating it with images from different tales. Make this your storytelling space, and fill it with soft cushions, toys and puppets that you can use in tales. Include a colourful storytelling mat, that you can both sit on when you read or tell a tale.

- As your child grows, she can use the mat as a spotlight for acting out stories. Keep a prop box in the corner, and fill it with objects and items that you can use to add colour and depth to your tales. Simple things like hats, boxes, pebbles and shells are all great tools for storytelling. They can be used as a prompt for a tale, or as an accessory with a little imagination. So a pebble is really a diamond, a twig is a magic wand, and a box is a cave where a tiny bear lives! Collect objects from shared experiences, so a day at the beach means you come back with shells and bright coloured stones for your box.

- If you start this process when your baby is born, it will soon become a ritual that your child enjoys.

Stories around the world

Or at least as far as the garden gate! Use your environment as inspiration for stories, and you'll be able to tell tales as you go about your daily business. Babies and young children need verbal stimulation and they love to hear your voice, so use your surroundings to come up with entertaining tales as you go!

Kitchen capers

The kitchen might seem boring and clinical to you, but look at it with fresh eyes. If you didn't know what the washing machine was for, you might wonder if it was some kind of portal to a new world. The way that it spins and whirls would probably mesmerize you. The same goes for the tumble dryer, or even the cooker, and what about the fridge? It's standing like a white tower. Is it a door to another world? Every time you open it, there's a golden glow and a faint humming sound. What could be inside?

- Use the things you do in the kitchen as a basis for a story. Washing up can easily be turned into an enchanting game:

  'Look how Mummy puts a dirty plate in the magical soapy water, she scrubs round and round, over and over, one two three times, make a wish, and look... the plate is all shiny again!'

- Make it a rhyme with actions and encourage your child to join in. It might seem repetitive to you, but he will enjoy getting involved in what you are doing, and you'll be introducing him to new language and experiences.

- Do the same with cooking. When you're preparing the food, pretend you're making food for a magical feast for a little princess. Start by saying, 'What would the little princess like to eat today? Let's see, here are her favourite foods...' and then list them. Talk about each food, describing the way each item looks and also the way it tastes. Then as you start preparing, talk about what you are doing;

'So to make this the best feast the princess has ever tasted, Daddy is going to chop the carrots, just like this, chop, chop, chop, chop... how many times did Daddy chop the carrots?'

- If your child is old enough include questions and counting games. You can even make up rhymes together:

  'So Daddy has a carrot, what will he do next? Will he chop it, one two three? Will he make a mess?'

Then move on to the next item:

'Daddy has some cabbage, what will he do next? Will he chop it one two three? Will he make a mess?'

Put in actions and encourage your child to clap the number of chops, this makes the rhyme interactive and gives them something to listen out for.

Bedtime stories

The bedroom is probably the place where you do the most storytelling, because it's natural to tell bedtime stories. Your baby will already be familiar with this room and the things in it. She will know that this room is a place to use the imagination, and share stories, and also a place where she is safe and loved.

- Use this to your advantage by introducing things into the room that you want to talk about. For example, if you want to get her used to the idea of having a pet, introduce a new soft toy, or a picture of the animal that you'd like as a pet. You can then use this in a bedtime story. Make a point of picking things up, or pointing out the pictures that you have put in her room and bringing them into the tale. You can do this with anything, so if you want to introduce new vocabulary, just place something in the bedroom in advance. Talk about it, and then use it in a bedtime story.

- Also use the landscape outside, so make a point of taking her to the window and talking about the view beyond the bedroom. Who lives there? Talk about all the little animals that go to sleep just like she does, and where they make their home. So you might say:

  'As baby goes to sleep at night, all tucked up snug and tight, so do all the little creatures outside. The little hedgehog babies are snuggled beneath that bush. The baby birds are sleeping too. They're hidden in the tree, or tucked up in their nest.'

- Show her these places, and make this a pre-bedtime ritual, so that she starts to identify it with bedtime and sleep. As she gets older encourage her to draw pictures for her bedroom. So she might have all the different sleeping spots of the little animals that live outside, you can then use them in stories and games.

- Take this a step further by making up a morning story, a tale that incorporates all the creatures mentioned at bedtime and what they do first thing in the morning. You might say:

  'As baby yawns and gets out of bed, so do all the little animals. One by one, they wake up. What do they do next? The hedgehog rolls over in the soil and sniffs the grass. The birds hop along the branch and chirp a little song...'

  Then you might say, *'And what does baby do? Baby giggles and he dances!'*

Toilet tales

The bathroom is a place where you can have fun with water.

- Start by simply talking about where the water goes and what adventures it has as it disappears down the plug hole. What about the toilet? What happens when we flush? Make up a story about a little person who gets flushed down the loo. Where do they end up? Perhaps there's a whole new world in the sewers, a world of wonderful creatures and people who live beneath the city streets.

- Remember to make this a happy tale and not something that will scare your child. The idea is that you're having fun, and introducing them to objects around the house.

Living room adventures

The living room is the place you all relax together. It is usually filled with comfy chairs and a television. Even if your child doesn't understand what's happening in the magic box (the television), he will by now have seen the images on it, and heard the strange sounds.

- Why not make up a story about it? Does it have lots of people who live inside and come out to play whenever baby appears? Perhaps your child could find himself magically transported inside the magic box, and in one of his favourite programmes. What would happen next?

- What about the sofa? Is it just a sofa? Think of it through the eyes of a small child. It probably looks like a mountain to them, so make it a giant play mountain with lots of friendly squishy cushions. Help your baby to climb the mountain. When they reach the top what do they see? You could even have their favourite toy waiting for them, so that they reach their destination, and they can relax and play.

- If you have the space, why not dedicate a place in your living room for creativity. Mark it out by having a colourful mat, and filling it with books and toys. Whenever you're going to get creative, you go to the mat together. Over time your baby will understand that this is the space for using his imagination, and you'll be able to put him there to play happily while you get on with other things.

Get going in the garden

The outside world is full of fabulous attractions. A journey into the garden can bring all sorts of weird and wonderful delights to your child's mind.

- Make sure you venture out at least once a week, or if you don't have a garden, make a point of going to the park, or a place where your child can experience nature. Try to imagine what it looks like through a child's eyes. It will seem like a magical wonderland to them. So tell them you're taking them on a trip into another world, a place where amazing creatures live, and lots of colourful flowers and plants.

- Start by describing what you see. Let them touch and feel things. Together get down on the grass and talk about how it feels. Reach out and stroke the bark of the tree, and talk about how old it might be, and the things it will have seen in its lifetime.

- If you have a favourite tree or flower, make up a story about them. Give them a magical power, the power to make everyone smile. So every time you go together to this tree, it makes you feel happy. Give it a name and talk about who lives there. Perhaps there's a wise old man living inside the tree and his job is to listen to all the people who walk by. Perhaps he collects their secrets, or grants their wishes?

Maybe there's a fairy that lives inside the petals of your favourite flower? She's so tiny that you cannot see her, but you know that she is there. Every time you walk past that flower, together you say hello and give her a wave.

- Think about the types of things you can collect from outside and use in your stories and games. Stones, once washed, can be painted and made to look like jewels or magical charms. Leaves can be used to decorate pictures and to draw around. Pine cones and acorns can both be used in stories, or as decorations. These sorts of items can also be added to your magical memory box (see page 89) as a stimulus for new ideas, though do make sure that babies don't have access to very small objects.

Creepy crawly heaven!

- Don't forget the insects. Go around the garden or park and point out all the things you can see, big and small. If your child is old enough you could make up an insect checklist with pictures of things they might find in the garden. They then have to find them and tick them off.

- Once they become acquainted with the different insects you can have a go at putting them in a story. Ask your child to pick one, and together give it a name and a character. Have fun imagining what the insect gets up to. What sort of adventures might they have? Play a game together and imagine what it would be like to be an insect. Get down on the ground and crawl like an ant, or wriggle like a worm.

- If you have a group of children playing outside, make up a game where you shout out creatures and they have to pretend to be them. So you might say 'Wriggle like a worm,' and then 'Fly like a butterfly,' or 'Jump like a frog.' Chop and change at different speeds to add a fun element, and give prizes for the best animal impression.

Travelling through time

Time travel is popular with children and adults – it appears in some of our best books and films. Babies will not understand the concept of time travel, but you can still use it in tales to introduce them to family members.

Grandparents

- Start with an old photo that includes grandparents and great grandparents, and use this as stimulus for a tale. Show your baby and point out all the different people. Talk about who they are and what they were doing on the day the photograph was taken.

- Treat the photo like a picture book and describe everything in lots of detail. Think about the story behind the picture. Why was it being taken? Perhaps it's to mark a special occasion like a birthday or a wedding, or maybe it's from a family day out. Describe what you see in a way that makes it real for your child. You might say:

'Oh look there's your great uncle swimming in the sea. I bet he's having lots of fun in the water just like you do when we go swimming. I wonder what else might be in the water with him? I wonder if there might be lots of fish?'

Or:
'Look at that big birthday cake. That looks just like the cake you had on your birthday. How many candles can you see, let's count them together...'

Time-travel story

- If your child is a bit older and understands the concept of looking back through time, make up a story where she goes back through time to meet some of the family members. So you might say:

'One day Molly was looking at an old photo of her great grandparents, when the strangest thing happened. There was a loud clap and a flash of light and she was sucked into the picture and back in time.'

- You can then talk about what happens next. Who does Molly meet first and what adventures does she have? If she's old enough encourage her to think about what she might see, and what sort of questions she might ask her great grandparents.

- Take her on a journey in time, and describe some of the differences from today. This type of storytelling opens the doors to the imagination, and it will also help her make sense of who she is and where she has come from. It's an exercise in social development and also a great bonding activity between parent and child.

Famous people and the history trail

Travelling through time in the stories you tell means that you can meet all sorts of interesting people, and you're not limited to any particular time period. There's so much scope and you can have lots of fun learning together.

- Pick a time period that you don't know much about, or even a famous person in history. Do some research on the Internet or at the library and find out lots of interesting facts about the person and the era that you can use in your storytelling session. Pictures help too, so if you can get your hands on some pictures of the person, then use these to help you tell the tale.

Time travel machine

- First you need a vehicle of some sort to help you travel back through time. To help you get into the spirit, set up a time travel machine in your living room, with the help of some strategically placed chairs. Drape some fabric over them, or do something to make them look different from how they normally appear.

- Together you and your child are now going to climb on the machine and travel back in time! Make this an event, by describing the machine. Perhaps it has lots of buttons and levers to pull. Spend a few moments twisting, turning and pulling various dials. Do a countdown in time, so you might say:

  'Mummy and Sameena knew they were going on an adventure. They could feel the time machine growl into action. They could hear a low humming sound, and it began to shake from side to side. Together they began to count down in time, ten, nine, eight, seven, six, five, four, three, two... one! Suddenly there was a loud clapping noise. They'd landed, but where were they?'

  Include lots of repetition and opportunities for your child to join in with sounds and movements.

- Finally decide on your destination. If you've done some research now is the time to get out those pictures, and use what you know to describe where you are. Think about who you want to meet. Perhaps you're going back in time to meet Florence Nightingale or Robin Hood? Ask your child to come up with three questions for each character. Perhaps they might want to take you both on a journey in their world. So Robin might take you to Sherwood Forest to meet the merry men.

- Remember, you can be creative and still throw in some facts. This type of activity is about using the imagination, making it real, and also learning something new. Your child will absorb more information if she really believes that she is there in the past. She will retain that information in the form of a memory which she can draw on at any time in the future.

- When you are ready, return to the time machine and travel back home. Go through the same process with the sounds and movements, and include the countdown, only this time count forwards, as you are going back to the future. Remember that young children look for familiarity and repetitive patterns, and this gives them the opportunity to get more involved in the story.

- Talk about what you have learnt together, and write the story up, as if you really have been on a fact-finding mission to the past. You can include pictures and rhymes to describe what you saw, and even make up a time travel log to record all your journeys and the things that you find out.

- It is important that your child sees you learning too. Not only does this provide her with a good role model, but it helps her appreciate lifelong learning and the fact that we never stop experiencing new things, and picking up information.

Look who's talking!

Encourage your child to get into the story by using familiar faces. This will help her connect to the tale and become involved in the activity.

Well-known characters

This is a very simple idea that you can incorporate into your storytelling and reading sessions. It works well with young children because it helps make the story real for them, by using characters that they are already familiar with.

- Pick a story. You can even use your child's favourite picture book, and add in someone that they know. It could be a family member or a friend from playgroup. The character doesn't have to play a big part. For example, if you take Nick Sharratt's book 'The Foggy Foggy Forest', as you turn each page, there's a silhouette of a creature or a person doing something wacky, and you have to guess from the shape what it is. So if you were going to add in a person you know, you could wait till the end and say:

   'Oh look. What a surprise! Here's someone we know in the foggy foggy forest. Who could it be? And what are they up to?'

   Then you could go through all the different people that it could be, and also come up with some silly suggestions for things that they might be doing.

- Similarly, you could take a classic fairy tale, and swap a character. So, for example, in Cinderella, why not make the fairy godmother, Grandma? Make this a fun guessing game, by swapping more characters in exchange for people you know. This type of activity will help your child make connections and it also makes the story interactive and fun.

Everyday experiences

- You can do exactly the same thing with everyday experiences. So instead of swapping characters you look at things that happen in the book, and swap them for things that your child has experienced. For example, if the characters in the book are playing football, but your child has only ever played 'catch' before then change the game. He'll be able to identify with the experience of playing catch, which means he'll be able to picture it in his mind. You can use this as springboard to explaining what football is.

- Consider all the activities that your child does at playgroup, and the things he encounters throughout the day and try to slip them into your storytelling. For example, you might be going for a walk and you see some workmen drilling the road. This is very noisy, but you explain to him what is happening and why they need to do it. Later that day you could be reading a book where the character goes on an adventure, and perhaps sees someone drilling a hole along the way. You can then remind him of the experience he had earlier, talking through what it looked and sounded like. By doing this you are helping him make sense of everyday activities.

- If you continue to do this with the stories you read and tell, you'll get to a point where your child can become involved and add in their ideas. So you might ask him what he's done at playgroup, or with Granny. You can then decide together if any of these activities could go in a story.

Make your own picture book

Once your child is used to adding in people that he knows and also activities and experiences, he will start to form stories by himself. He will be able to make up parts of the story, and you can piece them together to make up your own picture book.

- Start by deciding upon the characters including your child, any favourite characters he has, and also people he knows. Next decide upon what you are going to include by asking your child to think about his own experiences. What does he enjoy doing? What has he done this week that is new and exciting? What has he learnt? Make a list of the different things.

- Now decide who is going to do what. So you might have Grandpa learning to ride a bike, or little Arjun next door making hand paintings. To make this easier for your child, ask him to draw the illustrations. So you'll have a picture for each activity, and then a line beneath to explain what is happening. Highlight key words and rhyming phrases.

- Together read out what you have written and ask your child to describe what's happening in the picture. If you want, you can make a book with the pictures, or just keep them in your storytelling box so that you can dip into it at any time. Encourage your child to add in new bits of story every week.

Act it out!

- This is also something you can do with groups of children. Ask them to add in their own experiences and use characters that they know and together you can build one great big story. Ask them to act out the bits they have written, using movement and words.

- Or to make it really fun, put all the pictures and descriptions in a box, shuffle them up, and ask each child to pick one out. They then have to act this out, and everyone has to guess who the character might be, and what they are doing.

Recording tales

It's not always easy to slot in reading sessions when you've got a million and one things to do. But it doesn't mean that you can't do it. There are many ways that you can use modern technology to help. There are times when you could do with a story or two, to calm a situation. Perhaps when you're travelling in the car, and it's a long journey and you have two or three little ones, all vying for attention and getting equally bored. But of course you're stuck in the front seat driving, and it would be too distracting for you to start telling them a story. This is the perfect moment to stick on a tape of pre-recorded material. You might think this is cheating, but it doesn't matter, because it's all about the story and the sound of your voice. Here are some top tips for recording your own tales and making the most of this secret tool!

- Pick your child's favourite books. He may have heard them many times over, but that doesn't matter. The familiarity will help him connect with the tale and settle down.

- Don't go through the motions. Read the book as if you were really reading to your baby. Even better, record an actual story session that you can play back. All of your natural intonation and expression will then be caught on tape.

- Read slowly. You might feel like the story is dragging, but it won't come out that way when you play it. Linger over interesting words, and include as much repetition as you can.

- Allow pauses for a response. If there's a place in the story that you usually ask a question, include this in the recording. Ask the question and give plenty of time for the answers. You can always stop the tape, but you may not be in a position to do this, so put in all those natural pauses.

- Add in sound effects. This may sound corny while you're recording the story, but it will add an extra element of fun to the recording and give your child something to look out for. Before you put the tape on you will be able to tell her to listen out for any special effects, making the story more exciting.

- Include snippets of your child's favourite songs and rhymes. Break up the stories with some short bursts of poetry to keep her attention. Pick easy to repeat ditties that she can join in with. If you're going to be using the recording to help her sleep, then go for gentle rhymes, and lullabies.

- Get other people involved. Ask friends and family to contribute a tale or poem to the mix. This works particularly well with older relatives who might live far away. Ask them to record stories that you can play at bedtime. Make it even more interesting, by asking them to record their favourite children's story. They can introduce it by saying why they picked the story, and it will have more of an impact.

Film Star

- Have a go at filming yourself reading or telling a story to your child. This is something you can play to them at any time. You can also film them reading the story in different stages, or get them to join in with you. Make this an exciting experience, and act out the story together, or film them playing different characters.

- If you have a group of children get them to take different parts. If you haven't got a video camera, try taking photos as you go along. Then when you have a full set of photos, collect them together and use them as a storytelling tool. You can jumble them up and tell a different story or ask your child to put them together so that they form a storyboard for their favourite tale. Write captions beneath each one to make it easier for them to piece together.

Magical memory box

• Create a magical memory box that you can dip into with your child. Start when they're a baby, by choosing colourful pictures and photos that you can describe. Imagine that you are reading a story and include your child. For example:

'Once upon a time there lived a little princess called Zoe and she had a magical memory box. One day she picked out a picture of a beautiful garden. When she touched the picture with her tiny fingers, a sparkling light appeared and pulled the princess into the garden...'

• You can then go on to describe the scenery and all the things that Princess Zoe might encounter. Have fun with this, and point things out as you go. Initially your baby will not understand the words, but if you repeat this exercise, as she grows she will start to recognise things in the picture. Point out objects in the 'make believe' garden that exist in your own garden or the park. This will make the experience real for your child and help her make connections.

Developing the box

• As your child develops you will be able to invest more time in this activity by getting her involved. Let her help you decorate and add to the box. Start stories based on pictures and photos and ask your child what happens next. So when you reach the point of crisis (in the case of the story opposite when Princess Zoe gets pulled into the garden) ask her to draw a picture to describe the events that follow.

• This becomes a story-building process, because each picture can then be used to make up a new story.

• You can also include objects in your box that can be used to make up new stories. Shells, stones, cuddly toys, shapes, words and numbers make great building blocks for some wonderful interactive tales that provide your child with a unique learning experience. Don't be afraid to ask her what she thinks each object is, and what it is for. Always encourage her to use her imagination.

Themed boxes

• You don't have to stick to one box, you could have a few with different themes. You might have a 'Holiday box' with pictures and items relating to family holidays. A 'Birthday box' might include things from special birthdays, and a 'Family box' could include photos of family and important mementos that you can use to create exciting tales.

Props and characters

Using props and linking them to characters is a fun way for your child to become involved in storytelling. Dressing up is fun and it's a way to make stories more accessible.

A slipper for Cinders

This simple idea is something that you can develop, and that your baby will grow into.

- Start by picking a selection of simple tales. Fairy tales work well as they're easy for you to remember, and they include some great characters. You're going to create props and outfits for each tale. So for example, if you choose Cinderella, one of your props might be the glass slipper, so you might want to take an old shoe and decorate it. Or you might want to sew a cushion in the shape of a pumpkin.

- Think also about the characters in the book. What do they look like? Give each one an item of clothing or an object that defines them. For example, you might give the Fairy Godmother a wand, which could be made out of card or a twig. You might decide to give one of the Ugly Sisters a silly hat to wear, and maybe Cinders gets a woolly blanket as she sleeps on the floor in the dirt.

- If you want to make this easier, you can decide on one item of clothing and just make it different for each character. So perhaps a scarf or a hat, in which case you'd choose something suitably grand and over the top for the Ugly Sisters and something old and tatty for Cinders.

- Whatever you decide, these items should help you and your child distinguish between the characters. The idea is that you will use them as props as you tell the story. Encourage your child to become involved by touching and playing with them. Explain what they are and why you have chosen them. In time this will help your child understand the story and it also introduces them to new language.

- It doesn't matter if you can't get your hands on the right props, or if you're not very creative. The idea is that you take an everyday object, and encourage your child to use their imagination.

Drawer it out!

- The next stage is to create a box for your props. Or better still if you have an old set of drawers, devote each one to a different story. So you might have a drawer for Cinderella, one for Little Red Riding Hood and one for The Three Little Pigs. Decorate the drawers with pictures or stickers to show which story it relates to. You can also use this as a storage place for the books, with each in the relevant drawer. As your child grows he will associate the drawer or box with the tale and he'll be able to pick out the story he wants by choosing the drawer.

- Encourage your child to get involved and play one of the characters in the book. Make this a game of speed, so that as the character changes, you have to quickly find the right hat or object for the new character. This is great fun if you have a group of children together, as you can make it a race against time.

- Alternatively, try telling the story without words, and become the characters using the props and objects that you have. If your child is old enough he will be able to join in and create a narrative of what is happening. Finally, encourage him to add things to the drawer. This might be in the form of pictures or other objects that he wants each character to have. This helps to make the story personal for him and it is something that he can do over the years, so that ultimately you have the best collection of story props for each tale!

Storytelling games

This is something you can do with your child as she grows. Get her to pick her favourite picture book. You're going to create a game linked to the book. You can do this one of many ways. To start off with, try something simple.

Playing cards

- List the characters in the book, this works particularly well with books that have lots of animals in them. You're going to create some cards which have pictures of the characters on. Get your child to help you draw them. Try and draw two pictures of the same character so that you can play snap with your cards.

- Alternatively, write a number from one to ten beneath each of the pictures. There doesn't have to be any order to this, although if you want you could base it on the order they appear in the book. Now shuffle the cards up. When you're ready you each draw a card from the top of the pack. Have a go at describing the character that you have pulled out. Now place the cards face upwards. Whoever has the card with the highest number wins the pair. The object of the game is to win as many pairs as possible.

Guess who?

- Use your cards to play a guessing game. You each draw a card out of the pack, but don't reveal it. The object of the game is to guess which character the other player has. You can do this by asking five questions. With a slightly older child you could reduce the number of questions they have, as this will make it harder and it will make them think about the questions they use.

- If you have a group of children you can take this a step further. Ask each child to pick a character card, and then they have to be that character. They have one minute 'under the spotlight' when the other children get the chance to ask them questions and they must answer in character. This is a fun role-playing game.

Make the tasks related to the book. So if it's a number book, then the challenge might be counting, if it's a book introducing different letters then make the task about how each letter sounds and thinking of words that begin with that letter.

- Involve an older child in designing the game and let them come up with ideas. Working on something like this becomes an exercise in creativity and problem solving, and depending on the book and the game, it can include many important life skills.

Board games

- With an older child have a go at creating a board game for their favourite picture book. Start by deciding on the story, and then think about a large picture that you can draw together for the basic board game. Once you have done this, you will need to add some sort of path or trail around the picture. This is the route that each character will take to reach their desired destination.

- Obviously this works well if the book has some kind of quest theme, so for example with *The Gruffalo*, you might want to base the book on mouse's journey through the woods. At various points along the way he meets scary characters who might eat him, so mark these on your picture.

- Every time a character lands on one of these points they have to answer a question, or do a task related to that animal. This could be something simple like making the animal's sound for a young child, or for those a bit older, perhaps making up a short rhyme about the animal. The object of the game is to reach the Gruffalo's home at the end and avoid being eaten!

- Most picture books are easy to adapt into games if they have some sort of story, but even those that introduce words can be adapted. All you have to do is create a picture and a journey that begins with the roll of a dice. Then come up with a list of fun tasks at certain points on the board for each player to have a go at.

Set up a storytelling club

Hopefully by now you've got the bug, and you're using storytelling techniques in your reading sessions, and having a go at some of the activities in this book. But you can always take this a step further. Why not set up a regular storytelling/reading club with other parents and practitioners? Even if you only meet once a month, it's a great way to broaden your experience, and children will benefit from the range of different stories and voices that they encounter.

It is important for babies and young children to be exposed to different styles of language. In other words it's good for them to spend time with other adults, as well as other children, and hear the nuances in speech. They learn a great deal about the pattern of communication and where words sit, by hearing different types of language. We all have our own unique speech pattern and the way we phrase things. The more experience babies have of this, the more rounded their vocabulary will become and the easier they will find it to communicate.

Keep it simple

It doesn't have to be a large group, and the ages can vary, although it's probably best to keep within a three-year age gap, otherwise you may find you're holding some children back.

- Stick to a simple format. So start by playing an introductory game every time. This can be something as straightforward as saying your name and doing an action to go with it as you go around the circle. With babies you can help them clap and encourage them to make some noise. As they get familiar with the game, they will start to make sounds and movements, because they recognise what is coming.

- Introduce a fun element by using soft toys, or passing some kind of parcel around the group. Once you know everyone, encourage the children to point to different people and get the group to say their name and do the action. This is a great memory-building technique and helps to create a rapport.

- Next move on to story time. So that the children get exposed to different types of tales and voices, make a point of passing them around, so have different adults reading to different children at every session.

- If you want you can extend the time to ten minutes, and do some 'speed reading'. Have a bell or alarm to mark out three minute time slots, and when the time is up, each baby or child has to move on to a new adult and story. This gives an element of excitement to the session, and helps the children get used to the people in the group.

- When you've finished story time, bring the group back together for some storytelling. This is a chance for each adult to take a turn on the floor and have a go. Every week someone new should lead the session. They can read a picture book, or have a go at telling a story they've made up. The idea is that they will deliver the story, and then there will be some sort of follow-on activity that the group can do together.

- If in doubt, go for classic fairy tales, but instead of running through the entire story, stop at the point of crisis. Ask the group to decide what happens next and draw pictures to share. Depending on your age group you can get really creative and encourage them to act out the end of the story, or maybe become one of the characters in the book. Give about half an hour for this slot, so that the children have long enough to get into the activity, without losing interest.

- Always allow time at the end for everyone to share their ideas. This 'show and tell' slot is important because it teaches young children the importance of listening and respecting each other's opinions.

Tale swapping

- As you're ending the group, make time (about 5 minutes) for recommending any good books, stories or activities that you've tried. It's important for the adults to share experiences too. As individuals you will come across a broad range of books that you can use, and it will help you consider different types of stories.

- If you can, make it a book-swapping club. Every time you meet, everyone has to bring in a book. Pool your resources, and at the end everyone gets to go home with a new book.

- It will be even better if your local library lets you run the group there, because then you have the run of the children's section. Some libraries will be keen to get involved and recommend new releases, so make sure you ask for their help and input.

Letting the club evolve

- A storytelling club evolves naturally as the members get older. It doesn't have to stop once the children are school age. Think about giving the group a different theme every time they meet. For example, one week it might be pirates, and the next famous kings and queens.

- You can stick to the same format as before, splitting the hour between different stories and people, and making sure you have a session at the end that includes a group activity.

- Make the most of the mix of people in the group, by tapping into their areas of expertise. Find out what some of the adults do for a living. Or if they're from a particular ethnic group or culture, encourage them to bring along traditional tales. This usually leads to some wonderful memory tales, and an array of different cultural experiences.

- Storytelling clubs work whatever the age group, because they appeal to our basic instinct to bond, and appreciate tales, whether they're made up, or based on real experiences. All you need is a group of like-minded individuals, lots of children, and a mix of books. It's that easy!

Stories
for everyday routines

Stories and creative activities can be used to help young children understand the different situations and experiences they encounter as they grow up. Stories are wonderful tools for learning. They help children acclimatise to situations because as they engage with the tale, they become a part of it, and are able to identify with the characters. This kind of connection helps make the experience real for them. If you repeat this process then your child will soon learn what to expect and the situation becomes less daunting for them.

In this chapter I have chosen a handful of situations that parents and children deal with on a day-to-day basis. The processes involved are the same, and you will soon be able to adapt stories and activities for use in any situation. Experiment with this. Find out what works for you and your child. You will discover how they react to certain types of story, and what they feel comfortable with. Once you've got a creative formula that works, keeps using it! Remember repetition is the key to success when it comes to children's storytelling.

Bath time

Bath time should be fun, and another opportunity for you to bond with your baby and wind down. This isn't always the case. Some small children find this an uncomfortable experience and react against it. Whether your child's a water baby or not, use the following ideas to create a relaxing atmosphere that stimulates the imagination at the same time.

Bath time buddies

- Invest in a bath time buddy. This can be a floating duck/toy, or something simple like a foam sponge. Give the buddy a name, and begin by telling a tale about their adventures in the world of bath. For example:

  'Basil is baby's bath time buddy. He lives in the world of bath, where he plays all day and night.'

- As you begin to wash your child, continue the story, speaking slowly and gently as you go:

  'Basil loved playing in the world of bath, but he longed for someone else to play with. Then one day along came baby, and they played together for ages, splashing around in the soapy water.'

- Use your bath time buddy as a puppet to demonstrate actions in the tale, and play simple games of peek a boo with your little one while you are talking. If you get into a routine of using this creative game at every bath time, your baby will soon associate bathing with warm feelings of fun. They will benefit from the stream of vocabulary, and the soothing tone of your voice. This will also have a positive effect on their future language and communication skills.

Bath time adventures

- Make your bath a vessel for great adventures. Every time your child gets in, they are allowed to go anywhere. They can sail the sea, fly through the air, and even travel to magical lands. Ask them questions to get the ideas flowing, but let them tell you the story; where they go, what they see, who they meet and how they get home.

- You can make this a continuing tale so that every time they have a bath, they recount bits from the story with your help, and then make up something new.

- To help, draw up a story map together, placing pictures or symbols that represent places you have been. Make this a post-bath time activity, or use it as a lead into a bedtime story.

Water fun

- Use bath time to explore the notion of water. What does it feel like? Why does your child like it? Encourage him to come up with descriptive words and have a go at making a sing-song rhyme together. So if he says 'splash' then ask him what other words sound similar. It doesn't matter if he comes up with nonsense words, the idea is to get him vocalising sounds and exploring language.

- Give your child a funny phrase like 'Splish, splosh, splash,' and get him to repeat it and add a new word or sound on the end. He will enjoy the repetition, and this will soon become a bath time rhyming favourite!

Getting ready

Getting ready can often be a nightmare. Simple things like putting on shoes, tying laces and dressing your child, can turn into all out warfare if your baby has other things in mind!

Try using this as a time for some storytelling. This will calm you both down, and it's also an opportunity to boost vocabulary and help your baby understand the connection between objects and their meanings. Here are some ideas!

Shoe magic

- We all know the rhyme about the old woman who lived in a shoe, but how about giving your baby's footwear a magical makeover? Start by telling a story. Something simple like:

  'Here are baby's red shoes, one and two. These are baby's magic red shoes, because when Mummy puts them on baby's feet he is able to stand, run anywhere, and have lots of fun.'

- Take each shoe and as you put it on his feet continue the tale:

  'So this red shoe is for baby's right foot. This is the foot that baby likes to kick a football with.'

Do the same with the other shoe:

'So this is the red shoe for baby's left foot. This is the foot that baby likes to balance on.'

- When you've finished securing the shoes in place stand your baby up and add in some movement to turn the story into a fun game:

  'What will baby do first with his magic shoes on? Perhaps he will jump? Wheeeee! Perhaps he will fly? Wheeee! Perhaps he will dance and bounce? Wheeeee!'

- Your baby will enjoy the experience and look forward to the fun game at the end. This means that every time you produce a pair of shoes, he will be eager to get them on because he's anticipating what comes next.

Clothes horse

- To make getting ready an enjoyable experience, use each item of clothing to make up a magical creature. So you might start with socks:

  'Look at these white socks, they're made to keep your feet warm, but did you know in the magical land of clothes, they're used as floppy ears?'

  Then show your baby how they make a great pair of ears on you.

- Have fun and be creative with each item of clothing. For example, a T-shirt with a smiley face might be the face of the clothes creature; a pair of shorts might be the stubby legs and a hat might be the funny coloured hair. Demonstrate what each thing might be and add sound effects.

- Use descriptive words to describe things, such as:

  'This cap is really the green curly hair of a magic cloth creature. See how it sways and moves on his head.'

  There are no set rules to this, it's about making the unbelievable believable.

- When you've finished, come up with a name for your cloth creation. Explain that every time your baby puts on her dress she is stepping into the magical world of cloth creatures, because at the end of the day every item of clothing is precious and a delight to wear.

- You can use this type of storytelling activity every time you dress your baby, and come up with different types of creatures until you've built an entire kingdom of magical cloth beasts!

Stories for sleep

One of the hardest things to do is to encourage your baby to sleep. Whether it's winding him down at the end of the day, when you need some me-time, or soothing him back into sleep when he wakes in the early hours. Stories can really help.

When babies are very young the most important thing is the sound of your voice. As long as you adopt a gentle rhythmic tone, you'll soon be able to calm him down. As he gets older the story becomes more important and you need to choose tales that promote sleep, and have a slow soothing pace. Here are some ideas to try!

Night-time companion

- Invest in a night-time friend for your baby. Pick a small cuddly toy, something that he feels drawn to, and use this as a prompt for bedtime. So whenever it's time to sleep you reach for the toy. Tell a story about the toy. Maybe it comes from the land of sleep, and it's made a special journey into our world to keep your child company. It's a magic toy, because it's filled with sleep dust. So when you cuddle it, you immediately feel warm, secure and ready to drift off!

- Take this a step further by suggesting adventures that your baby can go on with the toy. Maybe whenever your baby dreams, he has actually stepped into the land of sleep, and his little toy helps him find his way back home.

- You can also use the toy to soothe away fears and bad dreams. So any nightmares cannot hurt him, because he has the magic sleep toy watching over him.

Sleepy rhymes

- Make up rhymes by picking melodic words that are associated with sleep. For example, you might say:

  'Nodding, plodding, drooping eyes. Softly, gently, flutterbys. Snoozing, sighing, curling toes. Snuggle, cuddle, into sleep he goes.'

- Repeat over and over, slowly reducing the sound of your voice until it's almost a whisper. If you have some soothing lullaby music you can play this too. A simple rhyme like this is easy to remember, so you can use it in the middle of the night to get your child back off to sleep quickly and without too much fuss.

Food fun

Getting your child to eat can be something of a marathon at times. With temper tantrums and food fights, mealtimes can go from being fun to stressful for both baby and parent. It's all about making food exciting, and engaging your child in the joy of eating. These creative ideas should make the experience enjoyable and successful for everyone!

Foodie playmate

- Introduce a foodie playmate; this can be a cuddly toy, puppet or doll. The key is to only bring the playmate out at mealtimes. Make a place at the table for the playmate, and give them a fun name like Milly the Muncher or Ned the Nibbler.

- Create a story as you go along by saying 'Milly is hungry just like baby. She says "What's for tea today Mummy?"' Then as you feed baby, you also go through the motions of feeding Milly making sure that you make it clear how much Milly is enjoying her food.

- Talk about the food that you're eating using Milly as a prop for questions. For example, Milly might point to a fruit or vegetable and ask what it is and where it grows. Use Milly to describe the food, and to talk about how delicious it is, 'Milly says yum yum, she can feel it in her tum!'

- This style of commentary using stories and descriptive words will inject some adventure into mealtimes. Food is still the focus and eating is the activity, but you can make this a playful experience and introduce your child to the delights of food, and the joy of being nourished and healthy.

Food characters

- As your child gets older you'll be introducing different types of food to her palette. To help this process, get pictures of the ingredients and bring them to life by making up characters, such as Tommy the tomato, Arnie the apple, Polly the potato and so on.

- Together make up poems about these foods, and to make it really fun think about all the ingredients in one dish. So if you're serving up spaghetti bolognaise, you'd include Sally Spaghetti, Tommy Tomato and Gary Garlic in your ditty.

- Stick to simple rhymes so you might say:

  'Sally and Tommy go hand in hand over to the frying pan. In jumps Gary with a 'wheeee', and altogether that makes three!'

Poorly stories

It can be hard for babies and young children to understand what's happening when they are ill. They can't express their frustrations like we can. They feel poorly but they don't know why. It can be quite a scary, isolating experience. So why not offer some comfort in the form of a tale or two?

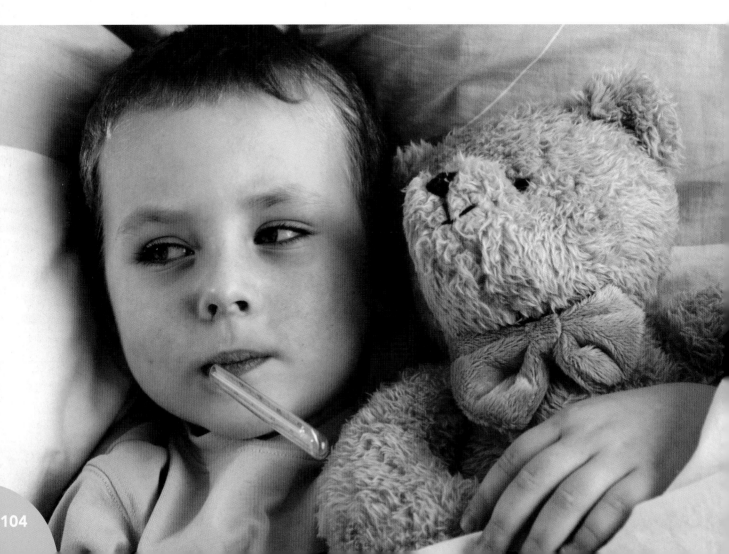

Sick buddy

- To stop your child feeling so alone and vulnerable, use a favourite cuddly toy as a poorly buddy. This will help them realise that it is normal to feel ill sometimes and that they are not on their own. So for example, you might choose Teddy, and maybe just like them, Teddy has a temperature and a sore throat. His head hurts, so to show this you might use a bandage. It's important to make the tale as visual as possible so that they can identify with what Teddy is going through.

- Put Teddy in your baby's arms, so that he can hold and comfort him.

- Start by saying:

  'Poor Teddy is not feeling well today. His head hurts and he has a very sore throat. What are we going to do? Perhaps we can keep him snug and warm and give him lots of hugs to make him feel better.'

  Demonstrate by hugging and kissing teddy and then doing the same with your child. Encourage him to comfort Teddy.

- Next pick a favourite book and say:

  'We're going to read this book together, you, me and teddy, and I bet by the time we've finished, we'll all be feeling better.'

- Once you've read the book, make a show of hugging and kissing Teddy and your baby, and encouraging him to do the same. Say:

  'Oh what was that Teddy? Did you say you were feeling a bit better? It must have been all those hugs and kisses and spending time together.'

- By using a poorly buddy in this way, you're helping your child understand what is happening. They no longer feel alone, and they are able to share the experience and also see a positive outcome.

Happy rhymes

- The best and most soothing medicine, is to make your child feel happy, and you can do this by making up a fun rhyme with a sprinkling of magic to help them get better. Start with something simple like:

  'Tim is feeling poorly, what are we to do?

  Make a wish for something nice, that's what we should do.

  Tim is feeling poorly, what are we to do?

  Ask the fairies for their help, that's what we should do.

  Tim is feeling poorly, what are we to do?

  Give him a kiss and cuddle, that's what we should do.'

  And so on...

- A simple rhyme like this will take your child's mind off their illness, particularly if you repeat it over and over again.

105

Separation tales

There comes a point in every baby's life when they have to be separated from Mum or Dad or both. This could be early on, when both parents have to go back to work. It may only be for a short period of time, but it's still enough to cause distress for both parties. The bond between parent and baby is strong, and when it's stretched, even temporarily, it can be hard for a young child to understand. Stories can help to prepare your child for this moment, and there are many brilliant picture books that deal with abandonment and separation issues in a gentle way.

'Owl Babies' which features in Chapter 2 (see page 56), is a good starting point. It's about a mother owl who has to go out hunting so that she can feed her baby owls. This means leaving them for short periods of time, which is fine when the babies are asleep, but when they wake up, they become anxious and frightened because they don't know where Mum is.

The story follows a simple pattern, as the babies wonder what to do. They are reassured at the end when mum re-appears and everything is fine. Just reading a book like this and highlighting the situation will help babies understand that Mummy or Daddy can't be around all the time. Here are some more creative tips to help.

Favourite toys

- Use favourite toys by making up stories in which the toy gets separated from your baby. Talk about how the toy feels, and turn it into a character. Explain that baby is playing in the other room with friends, and that he knows that toy is somewhere safe. Show baby returning to put toy to bed, and kiss him goodnight.

- Using a simple structure like this, over and over again, will help your child get used to unfamiliar situations. By putting your baby in the story, and using a toy that he is already attached to, you are creating a situation that he can experience in a safe environment through the medium of storytelling.

Make up a story

- Make up tales that put you both in the story, but include a point of crisis where you get separated. From this point baby has an adventure on his own. So you might start by saying,

'One day Mummy and Billy decide to go to the seaside. They find a lovely spot on the beach and Billy starts to build a sandcastle. When he turns to the left, he can't see mummy. When he turns to the right, he can't see mummy. Where can she be? Billy decides to look for her. He walks along the beach and meets a little crab. He says "Mr Crab, have you seen my Mummy?" Mr Crab shakes his head and claws, and says "Why don't you ask Mr Gull." So Billy walks a bit further along the beach where he finds Mr Gull. He says "Have you seen my Mummy?" Mr Gull squawks a bit and then he says "No, but why don't you ask Spotty the dog?"'

- You can then continue the story with baby Billy meeting lots of different characters on the beach. He might even have an adventure, or play in the sand, until eventually he realises that mummy was walking behind him all the time! Always make sure that you return to the status quo with a satisfying conclusion to the tale. Your baby will then know that, although mummy wasn't there for a while, everything was fine in the end.

Using stories where your baby finds himself in situations that are new and unusual will help with separation issues. Always make sure you put your child in the story. You can also use familiar surroundings, so you might choose the nursery or playgroup, but stretch the boundaries a little by having baby do something he's never done before. Start with the familiar, but then take him out of his comfort zone by introducing a new place or person.

Hide and seek

- Play hide and seek. Simple 'peek-a-boo' games where you or baby disappear are good fun, but they also have an element of separation. As your child gets older you can move on to hide and seek. Make sure you take it in turns so that you get a chance to hide and with every game take it a bit further. Rather than hiding in the same room, you might choose somewhere different in the house, so that you leave your child by themselves for a bit longer.

Mixing with other children

It can be difficult to encourage small children to mix, and leaving them for the first time at nursery is not easy, but there are ways to prepare them. Use stories to introduce the idea of going to nursery, and mixing with other children. There are lots of books that do this. All you need to look out for are tales that include children playing together, and having adventures.

Making it up!

Once you have read a book to introduce the idea of making friends, have a go at making up your own story. Personalise the tale and say exactly what you want to say. Here are some top tips.

- Make it really effective by including your child's name. If the central character is your baby it makes what happens more personal.

- Choose a setting that they are comfortable with. If you already go to a mother and baby group, make the story happen there. Your baby will already be familiar with the faces and the environment so it will be easier for her to identify with what you are saying.

- Introduce a problem or point of crisis. For example, your baby has gone along to playgroup with Mummy, but all of sudden Mummy has to leave her. Perhaps she has forgotten baby's favourite toy or book, so she goes back for it. What happens next? Who will your baby play with?

- Don't linger on the point of crisis. The idea is to introduce your baby to the situation without making him feel alarmed. So quickly resolve the problem and have your baby playing puppets with another baby, and having lots of fun. Perhaps she joins in the clapping game and when Mummy comes back she's really happy to have made lots of new friends.

- Always focus on the positive. The important thing is that the outcome is good and baby is happy. To reaffirm this, repeat key phrases and encourage her to join in. So you might say 'Baby's happy, clapping, counting, one two three, look at me!'

- Make this game part of the story and repeat as often as you can. If you do this your baby will start to associate this phrase with good feelings and you will be able to use it in other situations.

Going to the doctor

If it's daunting for us to visit the doctor, imagine how scary it must be for your baby. A baby might not be fully aware of what is going on, but as she develops she will recognise that she is in unfamiliar surroundings with strange people. Jabs, injections and check-ups are a part of growing up, but it can still be distressing. Use these storytelling techniques to help smooth the process.

Changing places

- Pick a character that you know your child likes. For example, it might be the mouse from *The Gruffalo*. Instead of reading the story, start with the book and point to the picture of the character. Say:

   'I'm going to tell you another tale today about this little mouse. In this tale the mouse has to go to see Doctor Mole, who lives in a hole beneath the earth.'

- Continue to describe mouse's journey to Doctor Mole's surgery. He's a bit scared, so to help him get over his fear, he makes up a little song. Pick something simple that you can chant softly, such as:

   'Come what may, I'm ok. See me smile for a while.'

- Repeat over and over again, and encourage your child to join in, with sounds and noises. When the mouse finds Doctor Mole, he has to have an injection. Explain that all he feels is a little nip in his tail and then it's all over. Finish the story by having mouse return to the woods feeling pleased with himself for overcoming his fear.

Make sure you tell this story a few times in the run up to your appointment. Soon your baby will associate the rhyme with feelings of safety and security. By connecting with the experience through the tale, your child will begin to develop a sense of familiarity with the situation so that when it arises in real life, she is more able to deal with it.

Make-believe surgery

- Help an older child to feel more comfortable about a visit to the doctors' by creating your own mini-surgery. Explain that your child is going to be playing the doctor today, and that some of her toys are feeling poorly. Line them up in the 'waiting room', and act out a scenario. So you might have Teddy Edward who has a sore throat. The buzzer goes and Teddy Edward enters:

   '"I don't feel well" says Teddy, "I have a sore throat. Can you help?"'

- It's now up to your child to help Teddy feel better by giving him some medicine. Go through this several times, so that your child can see that a visit to the doctors' is a good thing and will make her better.

109

Traditional tales from around the world

Traditional tales is a huge genre covering folk tales, fables and fairy tales; all of which work wonderfully with young children because they use characters that are easy to visualise. Don't be afraid to mix and match traditional tales from different cultures, as this broadens your child's general knowledge and helps them understand and connect with other cultures.

Personal, social and emotional development is key at this early stage of learning, and sharing tales about other lifestyles and racial groups helps children to appreciate and respect their differences. Tales from other countries can highlight similarities and build a common ground from which young children can take the first steps to making new friends. Not only that, but because so many of these tales are based upon moral lessons, children begin to learn about right and wrong. They can place themselves in the story, and make decisions just like the characters, learning through the experience of storytelling.

Do it yourself

- You don't have to stick to children's books. Do some investigation at your local library, and look into collections of folk tales from the around the world. Because of their simple format, you should be able to translate them into short tales that work with young children.

- Start by jotting down the premise of the tale. So for example it could be that the hero, a prince, hides in a cave from the evil king who is hunting him. A spider comes along and, recognising the good in our hero, decides to save the day by building a web in the entrance. The evil king passes the cave but because he can see that the spider's web has not been disturbed, he decides the prince cannot be hiding in there.

- The moral of the tale is that even something as small as a spider can be a hero.

Storyboard

- Now think of the tale in terms of a storyboard. This will help you remember the tale and also find the right words to use to describe what is happening. If it helps, actually have a go at drawing a basic storyboard. So come up with five or six small pictures to describe each step of the tale. Underneath each one, write a caption or sentence to explain what is happening. This doesn't have to be complicated, think of it in terms of newspapers headlines, and this will help you get to the point of what is happening using a few words. Setting the story out like this is almost like a child's picture book and it will help you capture the essence of the tale.

From memory

- Now have a go at telling the tale from memory. Think about your storyboard, and picture the tale like a film running through your mind. Go for simple language, and as you become more confident with what is happening in the tale, add in more colourful description.

- When you've been through this a few times, you will start to have set phrases that you rely on. To help, think of a fixed first line to introduce the story and how you want to end your tale. Remember that the first few sentences are about drawing in your audience, so you need something that will grab their attention.

- How you end the story is also important. It is at this point that you need to reinforce what the story is all about. So your last few sentences need to tie up the tale, and get the moral or message across.

Top tips

- If you are worried that you might go off on a tangent or forget the essential plot of the tale, develop a phrase or a couple of words to bring you back to the storyline.

- If it helps, split the original story into three parts, beginning, middle and end. Treat each segment of the story as a stepping stone, so the beginning is the first segment, then you have to think of a sentence or a few words to act as a bridge to the next segment.

Cultural tales

- When using stories from other cultures, introduce them by giving a bit of background about the tale. Where does it come from?

- Use puppets and toys to illustrate a point. You might take a toy and ask your child to use their imagination and see the toy as a young girl from the Amazon. The toy then tells the tale, making it easy for your child to relate to the story, and the main character. As he gets older, he will be able to take the toy and tell the story himself.

More ideas

- If you're struggling to find the right tale to read, pick something you already know well, and change the characters. So little Josh might become Ahmed and instead of getting lost in the woods, he might get lost in the jungle. It's the same basic tale, but with some tweaking you can give it a cultural flavour.

- Make up a game of chance to help you decide which culture you're going to concentrate on. Start by building up resources for a range of different countries and cultures. Gather books, pictures, toys and so on until you have a box filled with items that you can use.

- Next, create your game of chance. Create a spinning wheel with different cultures written around the sides, and see where the arrow lands. Or use dice, and make each number relate to a culture. If you want something simple just write the countries on pieces of paper, fold them up and stick them in a hat. Let your child pick out the paper and choose the country. As you go through each one, simply remove it from the hat so that you know you've covered it.

- Think outside of the box when it comes to activities linked to different cultures. If you are looking at African culture, and you've read a story and done some work with characters and pictures, the next step might be to do an activity related to that culture.

- Try making some masks together. Spirit masks are a popular way of worshipping the gods in Africa, and the people often make them to connect to their animal totem. Talk about the different animals your child might choose, and together make up your own spirit masks.

- Don't ignore other forms of creative expression. As you dig a little deeper you will find that many cultural tales are wrapped up in rhyming prose, or even songs and chants. Have fun with this and make up tunes for these songs and ditties. Come up with actions and movements that you can do with your child, that match the content.

- Make up your own songs and chants based on tales that you've read together. Take the essence of the tale, think about the key words and emotions and put them into a rhyme. Or if it's easier, give one of the characters a song or a rhyme that they can repeat over and over. This then becomes a part of the story, and something your child can join in with.